Cataloging Special Materials:

Critiques and Innovations

Edited by
Sanford Berman

ORYX PRESS
1986

Copyright © 1986 by
The Oryx Press
2214 North Central at Encanto
Phoenix, Arizona 85004-1483

Published simultaneously in Canada

Printed and Bound in the United States of America

∞ The paper used in this publication meets the minimum requirements of American National Standard for Information Science—Permanence of Paper for Printed Library Materials, ANSI Z39.48, 1984.

Library of Congress Cataloging-in-Publication Data

Cataloging special materials.

Includes bibliographies and index.
1. Cataloging of special collections in libraries.
2. Cataloging of non-book materials.   3. Libraries—Special collections.   I. Berman, Sanford, 1933–
Z693.C38   1986   025.3′4   86-2467
ISBN 0-89774-246-X

Table of Contents

Introduction

Ideally, professional codes and standards like *AACR2,* Library of Congress Classification, Dewey Decimal Classification, and Library of Congress subject headings should provide adequate instructions, notations, descriptors, and examples for handling *any* material a library needs to catalog. And, ideally, acceptable full copy should be available for most items from such services and utilities as OCLC, UTLAS, MARCFICHE, BIBLIOFILE, and LC itself. Ideally, yes. Actually, no. The Terrible Truth is that (a) some things (for instance, many local documents, small press publications, comic book series, and online databases) don't get cataloged at all; (b) the standards, codes, tools, and services frequently fail to account for certain characteristics peculiar to various formats and genres; and (c) the governing rules and national or regional processing centers often produce cataloging records that prove unhelpful to library staff and patrons, in fact thwarting access, promoting confusion, and contributing both to patron malaise and underuse of library resources.

In the original papers presented here, accomplished format and genre experts explore the problems and challenges of cataloging nine kinds of "special" materials: films and videos; computer software; Spanish-language works; comic books; children's literature; serials; fine arts; music; and government documents. The approach in each case is variously critical, practical, and creative, covering—as appropriate—descriptive and subject cataloging as well as classification and including numerous illustrations together with references to useful literature and other aids.

To begin, Jim Dwyer makes an amusing, but ultimately serious, plea for more user-friendly film and video cataloging, achievable through access-enhancing subject headings and added entries plus truly helpful annotations. Next, Susan Nesbitt contributes an urgently needed, succinct, and sensible guide to microcomputer software cataloging that can be instantly applied by those school, public, and other libraries now massively stocking software for both circulation and in-house use.

Arguing that for the growing number of Spanish-speaking library patrons to effectively use Spanish-language collections, "they must be provided with bibliographic access intelligible to them," Vivian M.

Pisano and Curtis Lavery raise several issues concerning the description and subject cataloging of Spanish-language materials, discuss in detail how to establish Spanish/Hispanic personal name headings, and furnish a bibliography of basic reference sources and cataloging tools.

Noting with some discouragement that over the past 50 years about 5,000 comic book titles have been published, but "American research libraries have done almost nothing to record the medium bibliographically," Randall Scott supplies an example-rich cataloging manual, supplemented by appropriate LCC expansions and a subject thesaurus developed at the Michigan State University libraries. The result of this pioneering effort should be the increased and more efficient use of comic collections for research and pleasure alike.

Holding that "to date, the profession's attempts at improving practices in the area of children's cataloging have failed to identify and explain the theory and knowledge base behind practice," Florence E. DeHart and Marylouise D. Meder first summarize the history of children's cataloging; then consider theory, objectives, the relationship to adult cataloging, and standardization; and finally posit important suggestions for research and reform.

"Librarians who have to handle serials daily," says Mary Ellen Soper, "either switch jobs quickly or develop a perverse pride in their wayward charges." And she convincingly explains why, examining in depth the special problems of serial frequency, title, description, classification, and subject access.

R. Cecilia Knight "addresses some of the idiosyncrasies in cataloging fine arts monographs," accenting classification, main entry choice, physical description, notes, and subject headings, while Don C. Seibert and Charles M. Herrold, Jr., chronicle the development of uniform titles for music, offering "some appraisals of the various formulations in terms of user convenience" and finally suggesting an imaginative "solution to the problems of user-inconvenience which were present with LC–1949 and *AACR1* and seem to have been multiplied by *AACR2*."

Ellen Gay Detlefsen doesn't merely bewail the second-class, haphazard treatment customarily accorded government documents, but rather states the case for maximum catalog access and even intershelving so that this increasingly valuable resource may be better exploited by staff and patrons alike. "Any library or information collection," she emphasizes, "can take at least some steps to improve access to government information."

Since many libraries subscribe to vital and costly online database services but few—if any—permit catalog access to them, Appendix A reproduces 25 Hennepin County Library catalog records that may serve as models elsewhere. Inasmuch as Florence DeHart, Marylouise Meder, and Mary Ellen Soper favorably mention Hennepin County Library subject headings, two final appendices contain selections of serial- and juvenile-related HCL rubrics.

List of Contributors

Sanford Berman, Head Cataloger at the Hennepin County (Minnesota) Library since 1973, is the author of *Prejudices and Antipathies: A Tract on the LC Subject Heads Concerning People* (Scarecrow Press, 1971) and *The Joy of Cataloging* (Oryx Press, 1981) as well as the editor of *Subject Cataloging: Critiques and Innovations* (Haworth Press, 1984). In 1981, he garnered the American Library Association's Margaret Mann Citation for "outstanding achievement in cataloging and classification."

Florence E. DeHart, a Professor at Emporia State University since 1973, teaches theory and application courses in the organization of information as well as a class on information transfer and special population groups. Her favorite library job was at Newark Public Library's Business Library where she worked half-time in reference and half-time revising and assigning subject headings. A current research project in collaboration with a professor of English involves young adult literature.

Ellen Gay Detlefsen is an Associate Professor at the University of Pittsburgh's School of Library and Information Science.

James R. Dwyer, Cataloging Coordinator at the Northern Arizona University Library since 1982, is a contributing editor to *Technicalities* and author of such pieces as "Ten Gators in Search of an Author with Money and Release Time," "Elvira and the Magic Sheepskin," and "Lost and Found in the Catalog." As Poet Laureate of Dexter, Oregon, in 1978, Dwyer asked, "Why can't librarians teach their systems how to speak?"

Charles M. Herrold, Jr. has been Music Cataloger at the Carnegie Library of Pittsburgh since 1982.

R. Cecilia Knight is currently the Audiovisual, Fine Arts, Education, Juvenile Materials, Library Science, and Generalia Cataloger for the University of Arizona Library in Tucson.

Curtis Lavery has worked in the area of international information development and multilingual access for more than 10 years and has taught both technical services and comparative studies in Latin

America and the United States. He is currently with the UTLAS Corporation.

Marylouise D. Meder, a Professor at Emporia State University (ESU) since 1971, has taught cataloging courses at three library schools. She started her cataloging career at Ohio State University and continued pondering problems of subject headings, rules of entry, and classification numbers as Head of Technical Services at Central Connecticut State University. Although her present assignment involves teaching reference courses, she maintains her interest in cataloging by collaborating with a colleague, Florence DeHart, on such articles as "Piaget, Picture Storybooks, and Subject Access" (*Technicalities,* 5, March 1985: 3–5, 16). She also contributed "Student Concerns in Choice of Library School" to the Summer 1980 *Journal of Education for Librarianship* (p. 3–24) and has written several essays on the history of ESU's library program.

Susan Nesbitt, until recently Audiovisual Cataloger at Hennepin County Library, is a frequent lecturer/instructor on software and other types of nonprint cataloging. Since 1983, she has worked on an American Library Association Subject Analysis Subcommittee, which will publish guidelines for subject cataloging microcomputer software. In her "spare" time, she tries to transform computerphobes into hackers.

Vivian M. Pisano spent five years with Hispanex as Project Coordinator, Data Base Manager, and, until most recently, Program Manager. She currently holds two half-time positions: at Stanford University Libraries as Original Cataloger of Spanish-language materials and at San Francisco Public Library as a Reference Librarian responsible for foreign-language collection development. For details on the Hispanic Information Exchange (604 William St., Oakland, CA 94612; 415-893-8702), whose services include current and retrospective bilingual cataloging, see "Hispanex: Serving Libraries Serving Hispanics," by Pisano and Brian Aveney, in the March 1985 *Wilson Library Bulletin,* p. 453–55.

Randall Scott, a Catalog Librarian at the Michigan State University Libraries, has devoted the last 10 years to the cause of collecting and cataloging comics material, and he is just getting started. Since 1979, he has been publishing the quarterly newsletter *Comic Art Collection,* which covers all aspects of public comics collecting. Lately he contributed two major articles on comic acquisitions and use to *Collection Building:* "The Comics Alternative," 6(2) (Summer 1984): p. 23–25 and "The Comix Alternative," 6(3) (Fall 1984): 34–36.

Don C. Seibert was a member of the Music Library Association's Cataloging Committee throughout the 1970s and served thrice during that time as chairperson, modeling his periodic reappointments on a musical form, the rondo. At present he chairs a renegade (though officially sanctioned) group within MLA called the Round Table on Alternative Approaches to Music Cataloging. He has been Music Librarian and/or Music Cataloger at Juilliard, State University of New York at Stony Brook, and (since 1968) Syracuse University. He regularly contributes interviews and reviews to *Fanfare* magazine, specializing in Tchaikovsky and other Russians.

Mary Ellen Soper, Assistant Professor at the Graduate School of Library and Information Science, University of Washington since 1972, teaches courses in technical services, including one dealing with organization of serials. She has written various articles on cataloging and is now working on a handbook of concepts. Before joining the Library School faculty, she was a serials librarian for four years.

Getting Down to the Reel Thing: Improved Access to Films and Videos through Subject Headings, Added Entries, and Annotations

by James R. Dwyer

Samantha Spade stared over the service desk at the egghead who had "scrambled" scribbled all over his face. While some media specialists may be hard-boiled types who don't crack at nothin', Samantha could be better described as poached: one of those goody-goodies who goes gooey over grumbling, garbling geeks. The poor prof scratched his dazzling, depilated dome, slammed the catalog drawer shut, and started to shuffle away. An open-and-shut case of the old Cataloging Casualty Caper.

"Excuse me, sir, did you find what you were looking for?"

"Actually, no. I'm going to a conference next week and need some films to show to my chemistry class in my absence, but the only thing I could find in your catalog was a film called *The Chemistry of Murder.* Frankly, my students are already complaining about what a killer class it is, so I thought I'd pass and just make a huge reading assignment."

"I know we have some chemistry films under more specific headings. Did you try looking under CATALYSIS, IMMUNOCHEMISTRY, or SPECTRUM ANALYSIS?"

"You mean you have films about those things?"

"Sure. COACERVATION, DISSOCIATION, and STEREOCHEMISTRY, too."

"Amazing. I would have never thought of looking for educational films under those kind of headings. I did try looking under EDUCATIONAL FILMS, though, and only found a book about making them."

"That's because we only supply subject headings for works about topics, not for examples of the topic."

"Well, you've certainly been a lot more helpful than the catalog was. Thanks a million."

After getting the films scheduled, Samantha thought back to her cataloging classes and the old principle of specificity in the assignment of subject headings—how using the most specific subject headings possible created the most effective subject access. . .at least that was the theory. For people working on dissertations, this approach seemed okay, but what about for most media center users? Could it be that following the course of specificity might actually be counterproductive?

While AV materials may be very useful to the specialist, particularly for demonstrations of techniques or depictions of physical phenomena, they are often used in a classroom or community group setting. Videotapes, increasingly popular in libraries, are used in both private and group settings. While a media production, like a book, may deal with a specific topic, it often touches on broader issues or subjects as well. For instance, a film on zoning regulations will also inevitably deal with land use planning in general. For this reason, it is advisable to consider the likely audience for a film and assign subject headings accordingly. In some cases, you may wish to add more general headings or additional specific ones dealing with a certain aspect of a film or video.

Library of Congress Subject Headings (*LCSH*), despite its many flaws,[1] does supply both specific and general headings. LC also supplies children's subject headings, and the *Sears* and *Hennepin County* thesauri should also be considered, depending on the nature of your operations and clientele.

———

The story you have just heard is true. Only the names have been changed to protect the innocent. My name is Friday, Thank God It's Friday, and I arrived on the scene three years ago. I could tell there was something fishy going on from the smell emanating from the card catalog in the Media Center. Then, about a year later, Samantha Spade showed up. She had a soft heart for the victims, but that just hid her steel resolve to make the Media Center safe for the user again.

When Sam and I realized what we were up against, we did the only thing that tough but right-thinking librarians could: we went to library school and found ourselves an intern. Then we put our heads together and looked at over a thousand card sets. No wonder it was such a mess: the minimalist media catalog policies of the past, the incredibly varied nature of OCLC member copy, and the principle of specificity itself had ganged up to stonewall the public. The catalog was taking the fifth.

It was obvious that we would have to improve subject access as part of our retrospective conversion process or else all we'd be doing would be letting the old cataloging go on the online lam forever. Out of those 1,000 titles, over 300 needed additional subject headings. (A list of examples is included as Exhibit 1.)

The most common problem was overspecificity (examples 1–5). We retained the specific headings but added more general ones which would help instructors find material relevant to their classes, headings like UNITED STATES--HISTORY, BIOLOGY, FORESTRY, and HOME ECONOMICS. In some cases, we added headings simply because the LC heading was obscure or overly technical (example 5); in others (examples 3,6,7,8), we added them to bring out a specific aspect of a work.

We also added headings for films and videos about individual authors and artists (example 9). Film is arguably a more effective medium than print for presentations of literature and art. In my own case, my love of poetry was both stimulated and encouraged by an incredible film about Theodore Roethke. Why did my sixth-grade teacher know about the film even though she was obviously not a Roethke scholar? Not because the film had the subject heading AMERICAN POETRY, but because the district media librarian was personally familiar with it. Since a librarian is not always available to help catalog users, it is imperative that we do a better job of gearing our cataloging to the likely audiences for AV resources.

Films may express as much through theme, mood, or point of view as they do through the pictorial or narrative treatment of a topic. A person might want to view something with a particular perspective: feminist, Christian, pacifist, Bahai, etc. Although some headings, such as BUDDHIST ETHICS, indicate a certain perspective, in most cases such adjectival modifications are not allowed, making a separate subject entry appropriate (example 10).

One might also wish to bring out headings that have a regional or local interest. In Ohio, INDIANS OF NORTH AMERICA--ARIZONA--RITES AND CEREMONIES may be perfectly sufficient, but here in Flagstaff we like knowing that the film includes Navajo, Apache, and Ute ceremonies. On the other hand, STEELWORKS--OHIO works fine here, but if I worked at the Sandusky Public Library and knew the film included coverage of that city, I would be sure to add a subdivision for Sandusky (example 11).

Finally, we added dozens of entries for *type* of film: documentaries, feature films, short films, experimental films, animation, etc. This practice is useful for identifying "entertainment films" which campus or community groups may wish to book and also for assisting communications students who wish to study specific examples of film types (example 12).

It is most encouraging that the Library of Congress seems to be paying more attention to such issues and to improving access to AV resources. In recent years they have been much more likely to add headings indicating genre or perspective. Unfortunately, though, they follow the principle of specificity to the point of wholly excluding general subject headings.

One might argue that adding lots of general headings will make the catalog larger, more unwieldy, and more difficult to use or, further, that the poor patron looking for a book will be buried in media citations. In a card catalog environment, one may wish to have a general catalog including all library collections and a special, additional catalog for media. If, indeed, the main subject catalog became clogged, a decision could be made to file the general media headings only in the media catalog. People wishing to book films or videotapes are likely to end up in the media section of the library at some point, and they are very likely to make use of a special catalog geared to their requirements and wishes.

In the online environment, this argument of "clogging" becomes absurd, since most systems allow searching modified by type of material. This feature of online catalogs calls the old theory of "recall vs. relevance" in searching into serious question. Numerous studies of online catalog use indicate that people take advantage of enhanced subject access and enriched records.

Recent LC records are also more likely to include the names of directors or production companies. Participants, however, are usually only listed in a credits note. *Coping with Technology* is a discussion between Buckminster Fuller, Robert Heilbroner, and Warren Bemis, three powerful and popular pundits who are not given added entries. Is a patron more likely to remember the exact title, the name of the production company, or Bucky Fuller? Likewise, a film about a person may include contributions by that person. In the case of the Roethke film, in which he both reads and discusses his poetry, both a subject and an author added entry are called for.

One should be particularly careful when reviewing older LC copy. Frank Capra directed several spectacular propaganda films during World War II, but the creator of such masterpieces as *It's a Wonderful Life* and *Mr. Smith Goes to Washington* is a *persona non cita* when it comes to those war films. Such Hollywood luminaries as Clark Gable, Jimmy Stewart, and Ronald Reagan also narrated films for the US War Department.[2]

Although LC media cataloging has been inconsistent over the years, member input to OCLC makes LC copy look more solid than the Rock of Gibraltar. Of the member-contributed copy we reviewed, more than half the records were unacceptable due to inaccurate descriptions, inadequate subject headings and added entries, and poorly written or cumbersome summaries. The same criticisms can be made of much of the cataloging supplied by media producers or commercial vendors. Such records should not be accepted by libraries without close review, and I encourage concerned librarians to partici-

pate in the OCLC Enhance and Upgrade programs or similar programs provided by other utilities.

Our findings are consistent with Nancy Olson's. She discovered
that media materials are cataloged according to a variety of codes (or
none at all), that various systems of subject access and classification
abounded, and that cataloging training was often minimal, with the
result that "there seemed to be some confusion between cataloging
and classification. . . .Some answers indicated little familiarity with
many of the terms used on the questionnaire."[3]

Printism, minimalist cataloging standards and training, and a low
priority for good public access to audiovisual materials seem to be
widespread ailments despite the continuing efforts of media advocates
to alleviate these conditions. Why should this be?

The first problem is simply one of workload and priorities. The
person assigned to do media cataloging often has a variety of other
assignments as well: public service, media repair, administration, and
cataloging "rush" books. Who has time to review cataloging? But, if
your library spends $500 on a film, you might consider the cost-
effectiveness of spending a few extra minutes to make sure that that
expensive resource gets to the people who want it.

Secondly, media cataloging is time-consuming. A film is not
scanned as easily as a book. Interpreting its contents may require
scheduling equipment and a preview room. Once again, though, time
spent providing quality access to an important and expensive resource is time very well spent.

A third problem is the proliferation of different cataloging rules:
AACR2, AECT (Association for Educational Communications and
Technology), Canadian, Bowker, etc. Even though *AACR2* is far from
perfect and extremely difficult to use—thanks to the hundreds of rule
interpretations and similar confusions emanating from the Library of
Congress—it is the most prevalent code in use today. Life would be a
lot simpler for media catalogers if LC would cease their meddling and
if other librarians would learn, understand, and apply *AACR2.*

Wait a minute. In the first scenario of this paper I said that you
should apply subject headings more liberally and with more local
variations and now I'm preaching common standards. Isn't this a
contradiction? Not at all. If you buy cataloging from a vendor, you
can modify it locally but you should keep some sort of local thesaurus
or authority list. In OCLC and most other utilities, one has the
ability to indicate what sort of subject headings are being used (*LC,
Sears,* local, etc.) through simple tagging. Catalogers from other libraries who may wish to use the record are alerted to check member-
generated headings against *LCSH, Hennepin County,* or whatever
other authority they may follow.

Tillin and Quinly observed that "considered departures from a
standard listing may be necessary in developing indexes adapted to
local needs and specialized collections."[4] The emergence of turnkey

and micro-based systems gives us the opportunity to customize local databases to best serve our clientele. Unfortunately, many systems available today lack the authority control power to make such improved access feasible, but we should expect considerable improvements in this area over the next few years.

Many of us face constraints imposed by lack of training, heavy workload, reliance on limited systems, etc., but our biggest problem may be attitudinal. We must make media cataloging a higher priority in order to improve access. If I could get one point across to beginning catalogers or media librarians, it would not have to do with rules, systems, or policies. Instead, I would ask them to take a few minutes to consider the potential audiences for the item at hand and then ask themselves, "If I were this person and I wanted to find this film, how might I locate it in the catalog?" With such understanding, assigning appropriate subject headings, added entries, and cross-references should proceed rather easily.

Catalogers with a public service attitude may find themselves frustrated by the limitations imposed by even an enhanced subject access system. They may wish to take one further step to help the client make the best choices. Catalogers of AV materials and children's literature have an opportunity for service and creativity through the writing of summaries or annotations.

Since films are not as quickly nor as easily perused as books, Ranganathan's directive to "save the time of the reader" (or viewer) is particularly relevant to audiovisual services. A class or community group doesn't want to wait until the middle of a one-hour video to find out it isn't really appropriate. Although there is no substitute for having the potential viewer preview a film, annotations can really help when a preview is not possible.

Subject headings often treat subjects as if they were isolated phenomena, and even if we apply multiple headings, we have not necessarily shown how those subjects relate to one another or how the form, theme, or mood of a presentation can affect our understanding of these subjects. Annotations provide us with just such an opportunity.

"1. UNITED STATES--ENERGY POLICY. 2. UNITED STATES--ECONOMIC CONDITIONS. 3. ATOMIC ENERGY--ECONOMIC ASPECTS. 4. RENEWABLE ENERGY RESOURCES--ECONOMIC ASPECTS" are all good subject tracings, and the assignment of four headings is better subject coverage than you will find for most films. But do you *really* know what the film is about? What if we also add this summary: "Commoner demonstrates how the US Dept. of Energy's emphasis on nuclear power is a drain on the US economy and how the situation could be improved through the development of alternative energy resources"? In only 33 words we can let the public know exactly what the film is about.

Since annotations are useful to the public and fun to write, one might expect that this would be a skill taught in library school, covered in the literature, and practiced with widespread expertise. This is far from the case. Of the catalog records we reviewed at Northern Arizona University, we found that 90% of the LC copy had useful summaries. This was true of less than half of the OCLC member-contributed copy. In many instances, the summaries were unclear, ungrammatical, verbose, confusing, or not even present in the record.

AACR2 provides copious instruction on how to correctly punctuate a cataloging record, but it mentions summaries almost in passing. Rule 7.7B17 states, "Give a brief objective summary of the contents of an item *unless* [emphasis mine] another part of the description provides enough information." In the words of Peggy Lee, "Is that all there is?" Although both are appropriately respected as cataloging experts and teachers, Olson and Frost[5] give summaries a similarly short shrift, while Weihs observes that films and videos "usually require description in a summary."[6] I would amend that "usually" to read "virtually always."

Daily referred to "the art of writing annotations" and sagely recommended that "a good way to begin the work of cataloging a motion picture is to write a one sentence description of the film and pick out the nouns as subject headings."[7] In other words, figure it out in English before you translate it into *LCSH*. While I endorse Daily's approach, I take issue with his observation that an annotation be around 100 words; keep it under 50.

Tillin and Quinly have written a fine statement on summaries:

The Summary provides a brief, accurate, and objective statement on the subject content of the work sufficient to guide the potential user in selection. The caption "SUMMARY" may be omitted.

The content should be summarized in fifty words or less. Avoid repeating the title and subtitle, or any information adequately expressed by them. Omit adjectives, adverbs, and statements which do not contribute to an understanding of the content, e.g., "This film shows. . .", ". . .tells the story of", etc. Always avoid promotional or evaluative phrases such as "an exciting film" or "an outstanding presentation". A succinct style is recommended, but clarity must not be sacrificed for brevity. Short phrases should be used when they will substitute adequately for complete sentences.

References to techniques used in the production (time lapse photography, slow motion photography, iconography, microphotography, animation, etc.) may be given when they are significant.

The Summary, together with the title and subtitle, should be sufficiently specific to guide the cataloger in the assignment of subject headings, and the user in the initial selection of appropriate material.[8]

This is obviously the work of experienced summary writers, but, judging from OCLC-contributed records, such writers are rare. Did all those English, History, and Liberal Arts majors who went to library school forget their mother tongue and devolve into mere computer hackers and bureaucrats? Perhaps they followed the OCLC *Audiovisual Media Format* which provides literally *no* guidance to summaries other than how to tag them. (You're it!)

The argument that such manuals rarely contain such guidance can be easily refuted by simply examining the sections covering call numbers, subject headings, and added entries. One assumes that manuals are used side by side with *AACR2,* but nothing plus nothing equals nothing.[9] OCLC could improve the quality of its most important asset, the online union catalog, by offering the sort of brief instruction that Tillin and Quinly provide. More to the point, there would be fewer garbage records and fewer multiple records if OCLC would only begin to load LC MARC AV tapes in a timely manner. OCLC might also consider monetary fines for the worst database polluters since the rest of us pay for their incompetence daily through the time-consuming processes of editing and filling out correction forms.

Exactly how do you improve local access to your valuable audiovisual resources through improved subject headings, added entries, summaries, and quality control? If you are a member of a utility, participate in its programs to improve the database. If you do original cataloging, do it right. If you have a local system, take advantage of whatever options it offers for enhanced access. If you rely on a district processing facility of a commercial vendor, communicate your concerns to them. Consider participating in a variety of ALA or state groups, AECT, or Online Audiovisual Catalogers. The latter group has only existed for about five years but in that short time has grown into a vibrant, active organization dedicated to better AV cataloging and improved public access. Such activity is beneficial to you, your library, your profession, and the general public.

It had been a long day in the city working the media beat. That's how Sam felt when she finally got home, beat. Time for a greasy sandwich, a cool brew, and a hot video. Sam shut down even before her VCR did, and as she drifted off, a sincere black-and-white image appeared on her internal viewscreen. A dream? A vision? A. . .a bibliographic record?

Wake up, Sam, it's turning into a nightmare! Next time remember the cardinal rules: never eat at a place called Mom's, never gamble with a guy named Doc, never catalog something without its audience in mind, and never, but never eat a hoagie an hour before bedtime.

```
Spade, Sam (Samantha)
     Sam's dream [dream] : better access. Everywhere : All
Catalogers and Media Specialists, 1985-
     At least 5 years : sd. col. ; all formats and sizes.
     Intended audience: All users.
     Credits: To those who improve access.
     Summary: Work individually and as a professional team to
improve access to media through improved subject headings, added
entries, annotations.
     1. Cataloging of non-book materials. 2. Subject headings.
3. Apes in motion pictures...
                         4. Baths in motion pictures...
                                      5. Charlie Chan films...
6. Disasters (DISASTERS!) in motion pictures...7. Our Gang films (NO!
NOT THAT!) 8. Repetition in motion pictures. 9. Repetition in motion
pictures. 9. Repetition in motion pictures. 9. Rep-rep-rep-rep...10.
Vampire films! 12. Violence (VIOLENCE!) in motion pictures...
```

EXHIBIT 1
Examples of Films and Videos Requiring Additional Access Points

1. *Baton defenses and techniques.*
EXISTING HEADINGS: 1. Truncheons [Rhymes with crunchin'. This is *not* a cheerleader film.] 2. Stick fighting.
HEADINGS ADDED: 3. Police training.
RATIONALE: This film is used in our criminal justice classes. We do not have any classes specifically dedicated to truncheons at this time.

2. *The Pomeroy file.*
EXISTING HEADS: 1. Privacy, Right of. 2. Pomeroy, Bob.
HEADINGS ADDED: 3. Civil rights--Case studies.
RATIONALE: Includes discussion of civil rights in general. A good case study for criminal justice, political science, and other classes.

3. *Born for hard luck: Peg Leg Sam Jackson.*
EXISTING HEADINGS: 1. Jackson, Sam. 2. Afro-American entertainers.
HEADINGS ADDED: 3. Blues (Songs, etc.) 4. Geriatrics--Case studies.
CROSS-REFERENCES ADDED: Peg Leg Sam; Sam, Peg Leg.
RATIONALE: I've been a Peg Leg Sam fan for 20 years and never knew, or cared, what his last name was, hence the cross-references. Sam is known and loved specifically as a blues artist and the sound track is pure country blues, justifying heading 3. Since he is a good case study of an active and creative octagenarian, the fourth heading provides access for geriatrics teachers and students.

4. *Sittin' on top of the world.*
EXISTING HEADINGS: 1. Old Time Fiddlers' Convention, Union Grove, N.C.
HEADINGS ADDED: 2. Bluegrass music.
RATIONALE: There are a lot more people who love bluegrass music than there are people who know the convention by name. (When do we leave?)

5. *When life begins.*
EXISTING HEADINGS: 1. Fetus. 2. Parturition.
HEADINGS ADDED: 3. Human reproduction. 4. Childbirth.
RATIONALE: Parturition? What sort of disease is that? "Did you know that over 90% of the children born in the US today have undergone parturition? Give generously, and we can end it in our lifetime."

6. *Chairmaker.*
EXISTING HEADINGS: 1. Chair-makers--Appalachian region. 2. Thompson, Dewey.
HEADINGS ADDED 3. Geriatrics--Case studies.
RATIONALE: The chairs take a back seat to their young-at-heart maker. Like many "Foxfire" type films, this is of equal interest to crafts and geriatrics groups.

7. *Silences.*
EXISTING HEADINGS: 1. World War, 1939–1945--Drama.
HEADINGS ADDED: 2. War--Moral and ethical aspects.
RATIONALE: According to the summary, this is "a film study of the moral ambiguities created by war." The setting of World War II is simply the background to present the issues. Could this heading be added to the "Rambo" films?

8. *El Norte.*
EXISTING HEADINGS: 1. Feature films. 2. Emigration and immigration--United States--Fiction. 3. Aliens, Illegal--United States--Fiction.
HEADINGS ADDED: 4. Central America--Social conditions--Fiction.
RATIONALE: The first quarter of this powerful film deals with the oppressive conditions in Central America that cause the migration. Remember, too, that some "facts" can be pretty fictitious and some fiction can be quite factual. The subdivision "Fiction" should not be interpreted as "nonfactual."

9. *My old man* [film of the Hemingway story, not the Joni Mitchell song].
EXISTING HEADINGS: No subjects. Author/title added entry for Hemingway.
HEADINGS ADDED: 1. American literature.
RATIONALE: This film is used in lit classes as an example of a film adaptation of a short story. We have also added appropriate literature headings to films about Dylan Thomas, Carl Sandburg, Edith Wharton, etc.

10. *Breaking out of the doll's house.*
EXISTING HEADINGS: 1. Short films. Author/title added entry for Ibsen's *Doll House*.
HEADINGS ADDED: 2. Feminist motion pictures.
RATIONALE: This is a film about feminism which has a feminist perspective. Either reason would be a good one for adding this heading.

11. *D.H. Lawrence in Taos.*
EXISTING HEADINGS: 1. Lawrence, D. H. (David Herbert), 1885–1930.
HEADINGS ADDED: 2. Taos, New Mexico--History.
RATIONALE: Includes footage of Taos when it was an artists' and authors' "colony." Heading also added due to regional interest.

12. *Time piece.*
EXISTING HEADINGS: 1. Executives--United States. 2. City and town life.
HEADINGS ADDED: 3. Animation (Cinematography).
RATIONALE: Provides access by type of film. Other examples include *Sky* (Cinematography, High speed), *Help! My snowman's burning down* (Experimental films), *Picasso* (Art in motion pictures. Cubism.), *Lapis* (Computer graphics), *Johnny Lingo* (Short film), and *Persona* (Feature film). The envelope please, and the winner is: the user! "I'd just like to thank all the catalogers and all the media librarians who made viewing this film possible. Thanks, especially to Sam Spade, Don Roberts, Nancy B. Olson, Sandy Berman, and so many others. . . . "

REFERENCES

1. Collections dealing with LCSH include Sanford Berman's *Prejudices and Antipathies* (Scarecrow, 1971) and *The Joy of Cataloging* (Oryx, 1981) and Joan Marshall's *On Equal Terms* (Neal-Schuman, 1977). The emergence of online catalogs has led to renewed interest in alternative approaches to subject access and indexing. *Information Technology and Libraries* (*ITAL*) often has technical articles on subject access.

2. Apparently this is the background in national defense that qualifies Mr. Reagan to be chief executive, much as his role as an informer in the blacklisting days makes him a champion of the Constitution.

3. Olson, Nancy B. *Cataloging of Audiovisual Materials: A Manual Based on AACR2.* (Mankato, MN: Minnesota Scholarly Press, 1981) p. 3.

4. Tillin, Alma M., and William J. Quinly. *Standards for Cataloging Nonprint Materials.* 4th ed. (Washington, DC: Association for Educational Communications and Technology, 1976) p. 25.

5. Olson, Nancy B. *Cataloging of Audiovisual Materials: A Manual Based on AACR2*, and Frost, Carolyn O. *Cataloging Nonbook Materials: Problems in Theory and Practice.* (Littleton, CO: Libraries Unlimited, 1983).

6. Weihs, Jean, et al. *Nonbook Materials: The Organization of Integrated Collections.* (Ottawa, ON: Canadian Library Association, 1979) p. 22.

7. Daily, Jay E. *Organizing Nonprint Materials: A Guide for Librarians.* (New York: Dekker, 1972) p. 55.

8. Tillin and Quinly, p. 23.

9. Rogers, JoAnn V. *Nonprint Cataloging for Multimedia Collections: A Guide Based on AACR2.* (Littleton, CO: Libraries Unlimited, 1982). Although I did not quote Rogers, I wanted to cite this book because I consider it the best of the audiovisual cataloging guides. The section on the user is particularly good. Interestingly enough, of the six guides cited here, five use the somewhat

disparaging terms "nonbook" or "nonprint" (meaning print is the norm)—and only Olson uses the less value-laden term "audiovisual."

Microcomputer Software Cataloging: A Practical Approach

by Susan Nesbitt

There are many approaches to cataloging any type of material, and microcomputer software is no exception. Individuals and committees in America and elsewhere have already written—or are currently preparing—a multitude of articles, rules, standards, and guidelines. But, in the end, the issue for every library—public, school, special, or academic—is whether or not the standards and guidelines really aid the cataloger and produce a bibliographic record helpful to users of the material.

The cataloging approach suggested here results from experience in cataloging a wide variety of software for public library circulation and general staff use. It is based on *AACR2,* "Guidelines for Using AACR2 Chapter 9 for Cataloging Microcomputer Software," *Library of Congress Subject Headings,* and the Dewey Decimal Classification System, but the decision-making process which generates cataloging rules and standards involves compromises which often sacrifice practicality for uniformity (or politics). Therefore, although formal cataloging standards provide a foundation for this approach, the final structure derives from experience and "workability" (for examples, see Exhibit 1).

Before a cataloger can begin to structure a bibliographic record for a new nonprint format, two issues need to be explored. First, the material should be looked at from the user's point of view: What do most users need to know about the item? How can this information be presented in the least confusing manner? THEN the cataloger can ask questions from a cataloger's viewpoint: How can this information be determined from the item to be cataloged? How is this format similar to other formats previously cataloged? How is it different?

USER'S POINT OF VIEW

Catalogers have learned from experience that users have a wide variety of information needs. Some may wish to scan the shelves for any title which catches their eye; others may be looking for a specific version of a specific work. The needs of public library patrons and staff have been emphasized in the examples in Exhibit 1. School libraries may need to specify grade level or learning objectives. Some special libraries may note price, size of packaging, color, or distributor's address—whatever information is commonly requested. In general, software, like films and recordings, is more difficult than print for the user to browse and requires more description in the record.

Once the content of the cataloging has been decided upon, the form should be shaped to clearly describe the item, avoiding vague abbreviations and obscure punctuation. Cataloging becomes merely an "intellectual exercise" if the intended audience can't recognize or comprehend the information.

CATALOGER'S POINT OF VIEW

Unfortunately, in the case of computer software, the initial focus has been on the issue of how software differs from other materials. Although the vocabulary and technology of the field are foreign to most catalogers, every nonprint format has its own particular vocabulary and technology. In many aspects, music and software cataloging are similar. The printed form of music is vastly different from its recorded form. A novice music cataloger must learn to recognize various types of instruments and musical structures and develop a whole new vocabulary. Novice software catalogers will also need to learn about various machines and applications and to develop a new vocabulary. Years of experience have taught catalogers how to create a bibliographic record which best describes a particular piece of music. Software catalogers can learn from these years of trial and error, creating their own workable pattern for software cataloging.

If the focus of cataloging procedures can be shifted from differences to similarities, the task will become less intimidating. The next sections discuss descriptive cataloging, subject analysis, added entries, and classification. In all areas, many similarities exist between software and other nonprint formats. The actual differences can be better dealt with when reduced to a manageable number.

DESCRIPTIVE CATALOGING

If at all possible, software should be loaded into the appropriate machine. This is not mandated by *AACR2* rules, but software producers often provide inadequate and/or inaccurate information on the package or in the documentation. Though it is unrealistic to expect that all catalogers will have access to all the machines on which the software they catalog is designed to run, a cataloger who *never* sees a piece of software in operation will be at the same disadvantage as "the blind men and the elephant." It is hard to describe the whole when all you see (or feel) is a small part.

Once the software has been loaded, some information should appear. It may be as complete as the title page of a book or it may appear on a series of screens similar to the opening frames of a film which only stay on the monitor for a moment, requiring that the cataloger speed read. (Film catalogers will already have perfected this skill.) Information not found on these opening screens can be taken from other sources in the order described in the Chapter 9 "Guidelines."

The paragraphs below address each element of a typical catalog record for software. Portions of an element which follow the basic rules of Chapter 9 are not repeated. Other portions of the description may differ a great deal from the *AACR2* recommendations. Individual catalogers may further vary their cataloging records to meet user needs. The following sample for a simple software bibliographic record and discussion of each element can be used as a starting point for most applications.

Sample Catalog Entry

```
Programmer/Creator.
     Title (Computer software). Version #.
Producer, date.

     # and type of carrier (Size of carrier, make of machine,
operating system, amount of memory). color. sound. # and type of
accompanying material. (series)

     Alternate title.
     Program language.
     SYSTEM REQUIREMENTS:
     CREDITS:
     SUMMARY: or PARTIAL CONTENTS: or CONTENTS:

     1. Subject--Software. 2. Subject--Software. 3. Type of
machine. I. Producer. II. Title: Alternate title.
```

Using this basic outline, a typical (if there is such a thing) software record could appear as follows:

```
Baumgarten, Sandra.
     Read-easy (Computer software). Version 2.0. Computer Easy,
copyright 1983.

     1 disk (5 1/4 inch, IBM PC, DOS 1.1, 64K). sound. color. 1
instruction card.

     Package subtitle: A reading practice game.
     SYSTEM REQUIREMENTS: Color/graphics board.
     SUMMARY: A self-paced reading practice game with over 60,000
sentences and 6 levels of play.

     1. Reading games--Software. 2. Educational games--Software. 3.
Reading comprehension--Computer-assisted instruction-- Software. 4.
IBM PC (Computer) software. I. Computer Easy. II. Title: Easy read.
```

Main Entry

Main entry is determined for software using *AACR2* guidelines created for other print and nonprint material. Some programs are completely written by one or two easily identified programmers and can be entered as such. Many other software packages will be entered under title due to the difficulty in determining primary responsibility. Credit should then be given to the major contributors in a "CREDITS:" note, e.g., CREDITS: Creators, Bank Street College of Education, Franklin E. Smith, Intentional Educations; original program, Gene Kusmiak; Commodore 64 version, Charles Olson.

If the title on the title frame differs from the package title, the package title should be included in a note, e.g., Package title: Lode runner.

General Material Designation

Chapter 9 "Guidelines" recommend using [machine readable data file]. This incomprehensible term is a good example of a committee compromise which serves no one. [Computer software] or [Microcomputer software] is a much more descriptive term and one more likely to be understood.

Edition

Version/release/update/edition information taken from the title frame should be recorded in the edition area. Documentation may show a different version because software is updated more often than its accompanying print material. Early versions of some programs have proven to contain major defects, and later program versions often make fuller use of a machine's capabilities. Version information can therefore be vital to a user.

It is tempting to make one record for all versions of the same program, but experience has shown that this is usually difficult. An early version of "Bank Street Writer" for the Apple II+ has 1 disk, a 45p. manual, and runs on 48K. The later edition, enhanced by Gordon Riggs, contains 2 disks, a 62p. manual, 1 quick start card, and requires 64K. Putting all this information in one record which will enable patrons to retrieve the version appropriate for their particular machines is an unenviable and counterproductive task.

Version statements which refer to the machine or operating system to which the program has been adapted should not appear in the edition area but should be included in a "CREDITS" note: e.g., CREDITS: CP/M version written by John Donahugh.

Versions for particular machines merit individual bibliographic records. It would be impossible to give an adequate description of the diverse machine requirements in one record. For example, although versions for various machines may carry a uniform title, only the "concept" is credited to the originator of the program. In the case of the arcade game "Miner 2049'er," Bill Hogue is credited as the originator of the program. However, other programmers have rewritten the program for adaptation to several machines, and two different companies have produced it. The result is a program which is similar in intent but far from an exact match between machines.

Producer

Like films, software may be produced by one company or individual, released by another, and distributed by a third. Credit should be given to each company if they can be identified. The larger company releasing the software is usually the one which should be traced in an added entry, because it is the one the public will know and look for in the catalog. However, some game creators have become popular, and although their programs have been sold to major companies and have undergone program "development," they should be traced along with the releasing company, e.g., Bill Hogue as well as Micro Fun or Reston Software for "Miner 2049'er."

Copyright, Printing Date

If the copyright and printing date are the same, record the one date without the word "copyright." If the dates differ, record both, e.g., 1984, copyright 1983.

Physical Description

Physical description is the software record element which created the most dissension in formulating the Chapter 9 "Guidelines." The current rule for physical description is to count program files or data files and the number and size of the carriers (disks, cartridges, cassettes, etc.) on which the files are recorded. Equating this rule to music, the resulting physical description for a phonograph record could be: 14 cuts recorded on 1 double-sided phonodisc. A similar print rule could produce this physical description: 23 chapters printed in one, 250-page book.

Even if program and data file information are useful to catalog searchers, this information is nearly impossible to calculate when cataloging commercial software. Most commercial software is copy-protected and does not allow the cataloger to "list" or "catalog" the program contents, the typical source of program, and data file information. Even if file information is available on the documentation, program and data files, like chapters in a book and cuts on a record, can vary enormously in size. Counting them is both difficult and meaningless. The AACR2 Joint Steering Committee is presently studying this issue, and it is hoped that more workable guidelines will emerge.

In general, a user needs the following information about the physical characteristics of a software package.

1. The number of carriers. The number upon which the program is recorded.
2. The type of carrier. *AACR2* recommends preceding all carrier descriptions with the word "computer," e.g., computer disk; computer cartridge; computer cassette. Using [Computer software] as the media designation automatically indicates that this is computer material and thus eliminates the need for this word in the physical description.
3. The size of the carrier. Chapter 9 "Guidelines" deal with measuring various carriers.
4. Machine type. If the software is designed to run on a "family" of machines such as the Apple II series, list Apple II or Apple II family. If it is designed to run on only one machine, such as the Commodore 64, list this.

For software that claims to be "IBM compatible" without being exclusive to the IBM machine, list as the machine type in the physical description: IBM compatible. This leaves the decision about whether or not the software will run on a particular machine to the machine owner.

5. Operating system. If this information is available, it should be included. Apple software written in CP/M, for instance, cannot be run on Apple systems unless a "CP/M board" has first been added to the machine. A machine without this board would not recognize software configured in CP/M. IBM software may require one of several disk operating systems which must be loaded into the machine prior to the software.

6. Amount of memory. Each computer is built with a certain capacity for storing and calculating information. This capacity can be expanded using additional hardware or expanded in later versions of a machine. Software programs are usually written to operate within the original capacity of the machine, e.g., most software for the Commodore 64 uses only 64K of memory.

   Larger, more complex programs require more memory capacity within a machine. It is important for users to know if a program requires more than the standard memory for their machines, because the program will not run if the memory capacity is inadequate.

7. Color or black and white display. This information is in addition to the System Requirements note which indicates if a color monitor is necessary. Some programs may be "written" using color, but they can run on a black and white (or green) monitor, just as a television program taped in color can be viewed in black and white. Other programs, such as "Rocky's Boots," cannot be used without a color monitor because color defines some of the options.

8. Sound. Some programs use sound for background effects. In other cases, such as "Bank Street Music Writer," the sound is an integral part of the program.

9. Accompanying material. Most commercial software comes with a variety of reference cards, manuals, and guides. Much of this material is essential to understanding the operation of the software. Material that will stay with the software should be included in the physical description.

10. Series. As with other print and nonprint material, some items are better known by the series than by the individual author or title. Weekly Reader Family Software is a type of software for the early elementary school child. Recording this series in parentheses after the physical description provides useful information in public and school libraries.

Notes

Most information about a piece of software is difficult for the catalog user to obtain by browsing through the documentation (if documentation is even available). Therefore, notes become a vital source of information and should be as complete as possible. Any standard note described in *AACR2* for nonprint material can be used if appropriate. The following notes are indispensable.

1. Alternate title: Used if package, label, or documentation title differs from screen title frame. This note may also indicate a "supplied" title if no title is indicated on the material.

2. Language: Used if the program is written in a language which is not included as part of the computer's standard memory (ROM) and must be loaded into the machine before the software. In this case, the language also becomes a system requirement and should be included in a note, e.g., SYSTEM REQUIREMENTS: Integer BASIC. Language information may also be included if the program is not copy-protected or if it is likely that the user may modify the program.

3. Credits: List here programmers, system designers, graphics designers, "creators," manual writers, etc. Some of the people listed in the credits—game designers/programmers, for instance—may be traced if prominently displayed and likely to be sought, e.g., CREDITS: Program author, Tom Snyder; story by Karen Eagan.

4. System Requirements: List here all hardware and software cited in the physical description that are not standard to the machine but which are *necessary* to run the software. As an example, for an Apple II system, it is assumed that the user has a keyboard, monochrome monitor, and one disk drive. Printers, color monitors, joysticks, second disk drives, extended memory boards, Koala pads, and programming languages such as Pascal or LOGO are all requirements which the Apple owner needs to know about, e.g., SYSTEM REQUIREMENTS: 80 column card and printer with graphics capability or SYSTEM REQUIREMENTS: IBM color/graphics board; color monitor; color printer.

5. Summary: If the software includes only one main program OR many (10+) programs, a general summary describing the main features of the program should be made, e.g., SUMMARY: Fantasy adventure using HiRes graphics which takes the player into a subterranean labyrinth to find lost treasure and fight off monsters; or SUMMARY: 32 "recipes" for calculating mortgages, interest rates, IRA income, and other monetary matters; for use in home financial decision making.

6. With: This note can be made in two instances: if the software includes two main programs and the first program is used as the main entry or if the software has one version on one side of the disk and a second version on the other. In either instance, a SUMMARY note should be made for the program listed as the main entry and a WITH statement should be made for the information about the second program or side, e.g., SUMMARY: Simple home word processing program which includes preset forms for outlines, resumes, envelopes, and memos; and WITH: Spelling dictionary to verify words used in files created by the word processing program. Or SUMMARY: Arcade game which matches a melon farmer against bouncing furballs that rain from the sky and try to mash ripe melons; and WITH: Apple II version on side 2.

7. Contents/Partial Contents: Used if the software includes several major programs. List all by title, each followed in parentheses by a short description, e.g., CONTENTS: Find your number (Number guessing game). -Find the Bumble (Graph reading game). -Butterfly hunt (Graph reading game). -Visit from space (Graph reading game). -Tic tac toc (Variation of tic tac toe).

It may not be necessary to list all of the titles, such as "Introduction" or "program descriptions," in which case a partial contents note may be made, e.g., PARTIAL CONTENTS: Furs (Fur trading expedition simulation). -Nomad (Map reading game). -Oregon (Westward migration simulation). -Sumeria (Ancient kingdom simulation). -Voyageur (Fur trade simulation).

Where contents titles are self-descriptive, the summary in parentheses may not be necessary, e.g., PARTIAL CONTENTS: Calendar. -Address file. -Shopping list. -Recipe file.

Chapter 9 recommends listing in a note machines on which the software *may* also run. This can be an endless task due to the increasing sophistication of software and machines. It also creates difficulties in determining the system requirements for these other machines as they may differ in the amount of standard memory, number of built-in disk drives, disk operating system, etc. In situations where the software is to be used on only a few set machines, however, the "also runs on" note could be useful. A special library checking out software for IBM PCs and Osbournes may include a note such as: "Also runs on Osbourne II with 64K and CP/M 2.2."

SUBJECT ANALYSIS

In many instances, the catalog user searching for information about a piece of software is more knowledgeable about the field than the cataloger who created the record. It is necessary, then, not to underestimate the level of sophistication in subject analysis the user may expect.

Each piece of software should undergo subject analysis equal to or greater than that given to other print and nonprint material. As with notes, catalogers should be generous in assigning subject headings due to the difficulty of determining content by browsing. Five main points to keep in mind when subject analyzing software follow.

1. The *content* or *subject* of a piece of software should take precedence over the form. Films about gardening are given the subject heading GARDENING with any appropriate subdivisions, rather than FILMS--GARDENING. A video tape on golf gets the heading GOLF rather than VIDEO TAPES--GOLF. Software also deals with a variety of subjects and should get headings like WORD PROCESSING--SOFTWARE and INTEREST RATES--CALCULATION--COMPUTER METHODS--SOFTWARE.

2. Experience shows that catalog entries for software are searched on two levels: specific title or topic, e.g., The story machine; SHORT STORY WRITING--COMPUTER METHODS--SOFTWARE or more general applications or "genre" groupings like EDUCATIONAL SOFTWARE, ARCADE GAMES--SOFTWARE, and PRESCHOOLERS' SOFTWARE. Catalogers need to be sensitive to both levels of searches and provide adequate access.

3. Libraries which catalog software for more than one machine will find demand for a genre heading by machine. The genre heading should follow the form established by the Library of Congress in its *Weekly Lists* followed by "software." Use the minimum type or family of machine or operating system on which the software will run. If it will run on an Apple II+, IIe, and IIc, trace as follows: APPLE II (COMPUTER) SOFTWARE. If it will only run on the IIc, use the tracing: APPLE IIc (COMPUTER) SOFTWARE. Do not trace machines on which the software will run if they need to be modified unless those modifications are specified in the SYSTEM REQUIREMENTS note, e.g., 1. Commodore 64 (Computer) software.

4. The subheading --SOFTWARE should be applied to all subject headings attached to software records. The Library of Congress applies the subheading --COMPUTER PROGRAMS to the printed version of software. Applying the subheading --SOFTWARE to the machine version of the program will make it much easier to distinguish between the two versions.

5. Software often does more than simply furnish information about a topic. It is usually designed to calculate, construct, simulate, or instruct. Using subheadings to define the action of the software helps to more correctly describe it, e.g., TYPEWRITING--

COMPUTER-ASSISTED INSTRUCTION--SOFTWARE; COM-
PARISON SHOPPING--COMPUTER SIMULATION--SOFT-
WARE; CROSSWORD PUZZLES--CONSTRUCTION--COM-
PUTER METHODS--SOFTWARE; MORTGAGES--CALCULA-
TION--COMPUTER METHODS--SOFTWARE.

With these points in mind, subject analysis can begin. Running
the program and/or reading documentation and reviews should help
determine subject content. Once the subject (or subjects) has been
determined, the cataloger must create headings which best describe
the topic. Although the Library of Congress has cataloged some books
about specific programs, it has not yet begun to catalog software. This
fact makes Library of Congress Subject Headings—fiche, print, or
weekly lists—even less useful for software than for other audiovisual
material. The *Weekly Lists* (although far behind in publication) are a
good source for establishing uniform names for computers. Most
catalogers, however, will need to find a source for new headings *and*
learn to create, cross-reference, and document headings of their own.

Some school and state libraries have established software cataloging consortiums and may be willing to share their subject authority
lists. Hennepin County Library has a reference and circulating collection of several hundred pieces of software. The subject headings and
cross references assigned to this software are available as part of a
quarterly authority file on microfiche and are reported bimonthly in
the *Hennepin County Library Cataloging Bulletin.*

No matter which authority list a cataloger uses as a reference, it
will become necessary at some point to create new subject headings.
The most readily available sources for new subject headings are the
software menu, introduction, documentation, and packaging information. Further validation for newly created terms can be found in
indexes such as the *Microcomputer Index*; *The Software Catalog:
Microcomputers, National Education Association Yellow Book, The
Parent-Teacher's Microcomputing Sourcebook for Children,* and other
directories; computer glossaries and dictionaries like *The Computer
Cookbook*; and reviews and advertising found in *InfoWorld, A+, Personal Computing,* and similar popular periodicals.

Using current, popular sources as references will help the cataloger avoid the pitfall of choosing outdated or overgeneralized terminology. Current and popular sources will also supply examples for
"genre" headings such as INTERACTIVE FICTION or SCIENCE
FICTION ADVENTURE GAMES and provide information for summary statements.

Once a subject heading has been created, it must be integrated
into the subject hierarchy and given appropriate cross references and
scope notes. Examples of new subject headings with appropriate cross
references and scope notes can be found in Exhibit 2.

ADDED ENTRIES

Added entries should be made for software on the same basis as for other print and audiovisual material. Usually, however, make an added entry for the following items.

1. <u>Main publisher.</u> Access to all software the library carries produced by a popular company is a common request, e.g., II. Spinnaker Software. III. Electronic Arts.
2. <u>Programmer or designer of some games or educational programs.</u> For example, IV. Budge, Bill. V. Snyder, Tom.
3. <u>Titles of popular games.</u> Those which are not the main title entry but which were cited in CONTENTS, PARTIAL CONTENTS, or WITH notes and are likely to be sought by catalog users, e.g., CONTENTS: Caterpillar (Alphabet drill). -Pictures (Reading game). -Wuzzle (Counting drill). . . .I. Title: Caterpillar. II. Title: Wuzzle.
4. <u>Series.</u> Use the series tracing to draw together in the catalog titles which are sequential or closely related but which would not necessarily file adjacent to one another otherwise. The MECC elementary series begins with pre-reading and counting skills in the early volumes and continues on to upper elementary science and social studies in the later volumes. Tracing the numbered series will gather all of the volumes together in order in the catalog, e.g., I. Series: MECC Elementary Series, volume 1. In some situations, it may also be useful to trace some or all publishers' series, e.g., Weekly Reader Family Software; Barron's Educational Software.

CLASSIFICATION

Software should be integrated into the total collection. After determining the subject content, classification should follow the same guidelines as other print and audiovisual material. Software dealing with specific subjects should be classed within those subject number ranges, e.g., Chocolate Bytes (a recipe file) in 641.6347; Dinosaurs in 568.19 (HCL number) or 567.91 (DDC 19).

Only programming tutorials, communications and networking software, or disk utilities and operating systems should be classed in the data processing numbers. The new Dewey Decimal Classification schedules for "004-006 Data Processing and Computer Science" have alleviated the task of arranging these types of software by greatly expanding the range of numbers out of the 001.64's into a previously unused range.

Some examples of new numbers in these schedules which will facilitate shelf browsing:

006.686 Graphics programs for digital microcomputers.

005.7565 Specific relational database management systems (arranged alphabetically by name of program).

005.43 Systems programs/Operating systems (including utility programs).

005.71 Data communications (including software for interfacing and operating modems).

The new schedules also contain a good index and glossary which may be very helpful to a cataloger unfamiliar with computer terminology.

It is an exciting time to be cataloging software. The rules are still being written. Creative solutions are being sought. New approaches can be tried. User-oriented cataloging can become the norm.

Every day computer capabilities are expanding and new types of software are being developed. It is a challenge to catalogers to keep pace with the field. It is more necessary than ever for catalogers to share experiences and ideas. Please share *your* ideas, comments, and questions with me:

Susan Nesbitt
Community Services Management and Planning Division
A-1008 Hennepin County Government Center
Minneapolis, MN 55487

EXHIBIT 1
Examples

```
CS Commodore 781.61C

Clancy, Glen.

      Bank Street music writer (Computer software). Mindscape, copyright
1985.

      1 disk (5 1/4 inch, Commodore 64). sound. color. 1 reference card.
1 manual (64p.). (Folio series)

      CREDITS: Developed by the Bank Street College of Education.
      SUMMARY: Enables a composer to write and edit music from simple
melodies to three-part compositions, with playback and printing
capabilities.

      1. Music composition--Software. 2. Computer music--Software.
3. Commodore 64 (Computer) software. I. Bank Street College of
Education, New York. II. Mindscape. III. Title: Music writer. IV.
Title.
```

CS IBM 629.13252A

Artwick, Bruce.

    Flight simulator (Computer software). Microsoft, copyright 1984.

    1 disk (5 1/4 inch, IBM PC, DOS 2.2, 128K). sound. color. 1
handbook (149p.).

    SYSTEM REQUIREMENTS: Color/graphics board.
    SUMMARY: A simulation program which puts the player in the pilot's
seat of a Cessna 82 class and includes the "World War I Ace" aerial
battle game.

    1. War games--Computer simulation--Software. 2. Flight--Computer
simulation--Software. 3. Computer games--Software. 4. IBM PC (Computer)
software. I. Microsoft. II. Title.

CS Apple 004F

    The Friendly computer (Computer software). Version 1.1.
Minnesota Educational Computing Consortium, copyright 1984.

    1 disk (5 1/4 inch, Apple II series, DOS 3.3, 48K). 1
manual (unpaged).

    CONTENTS: Keyboard (Key location). -Zebug (Key location games).
Term worm (Computer animation teaches parts of a computer). -Picture
(Create and save drawings). -Picture show (Displays pictures saved from
Picture file).

    1. Computers--Terminology--Computer-assisted instruction
(Elementary)--Software. 2. Computer literacy--Computer-assisted
instruction (Elementary)--Software. 3. Computer drawing--Software. 4.
Computer art--Software. 5. Educational software. 6. Apple II (Computer)
software. I. MECC. II. Title: Zebug.

CS Commodore 794.82D

Denman, William F.
    Pogo Joe (Computer software). By William F. Denman and Oliver W.
Steele. Screenplay, copyright 1983.

    1 cassette (Commodore 64). sound. color. 1 guide card.

    SYSTEM REQUIREMENTS: Joystick.
    SUMMARY: Arcade game in which Pogo Joe jumps from cylinder to
cylinder trying to avoid various toy monsters.

    1. Arcade games--Software. 2. Computer games--Software. 3.
Commodore 64 (Computer) software. I. Steele, Oliver W. II. Screenplay.
II. Title.

EXHIBIT 2
Subject Headings: A Selection

Key

Assignment. Title and producer of software package to which the subject heading has first been assigned.

cn. Cataloger's note which appears in the authority file as cataloging information but not in the bibliographic record or in the catalog.

pn. Public (or scope) note which appears in the catalog under a subject heading when the definition of the term may be otherwise unclear.

sa. See also, used to indicate narrower terms which are related to the broader subject heading and may also be sought by catalog users.

sf. See from, employed for unused synonymous, inverted, or misspelled terms which direct the searcher to the correct term.

Adventure games--Software.
      Assignment: Infidel, by Infocom.
      cn   HCL form. Make dual entry under COMPUTER GAMES--SOFTWARE.
      pn   Here is entered software for computer games in which the player moves through a series of rooms or screens while solving problems and facing challenges produced by the computer, depending on the player's choices.
      sa   Fantasy adventure games--Software. Mystery adventure games--Software. Science fiction adventure games--Software.

Alphabet games--Software.
      Assignment: Stickybear ABC, by Optimum Resource.
      cn   Make dual entry under EDUCATIONAL GAMES--SOFTWARE.

Arcade games--Software.
      Assignment: Lode runner, by Broderbund.
      cn   Make dual entry under COMPUTER GAMES--SOFTWARE.

Banners--Construction--Computer Methods--Software.
      Assignment: Puzzles and posters, by MECC.

Communications software.
>Assignment: ASCII Express, by United SWI.
>pn   Here is entered software which facilitates modem connections and data transmission.
>sf   Microcomputer communications software.

Computer art--Software.
>Assignment: Kaleida, by Once Begun Computations.
>pn   Here is entered software which uses computer graphics to produce artistic pictures and designs.
>sa   Computer drawing--Software. Computer graphics--Software.
>sf   Art, Computer--Software.

Computer drawing--Software.
>Assignment: Delta Drawing, by Spinnaker.
>pn   Here is entered software which uses keyboard commands, joystick, mouse, or KOALA pad to produce line drawings.
>sf   Drawing, Computer--Software.

Computer games--Software.
>sa   Adventure games--Software. Arcade games--Software. Chess--Software. Computer games--Programs. Contract bridge--Software. Educational games--Software. Pinball--Software. Sports games--Software. Trivia games--Software. War games--Software.

Computer games--design--Software.
>Assignment: Pinball construction set, by Electronic Arts.
>sf   Computer games--Construction--Software.

Computer graphics--Software.
>Assignment: The print shop graphics library, volume 1, by Broderbund.
>sa   Computer art--Software. Turtle graphics--Software.

Computer literacy--Computer-assisted instruction--Software.
>Assignment: Rocky's Boots, by Learning Company.
>pn   Here is entered software which teaches the use, capabilities, applications, and/or social implications of a computer.

Computer printing--Software.
>Assignment: The print shop graphics library, volume 1, by Broderbund.
>sa   Mailing labels--Production--Computer Methods--Software.

Counting games--Software.
>Assignment: Stickybear numbers, by Optimum Resources.
>cn   Make dual entry under EDUCATIONAL GAMES--SOFTWARE.

Crossword puzzles--Construction--Computer Methods--Software.
>Assignment: Puzzles and posters, by MECC.

Database management--Software.
>Assignment: Data handler, by MECC.
>pn   Here is entered software which can create, search, and edit a database.

Databases--Reporting--Software.
>Assignment: PFS Report, by Software Publishing.
>pn   Here is entered software which can format, edit, and print database files.

Desktop management--Software.
>Assignment: Sidekick, by Borland International.
>pn   Here is entered a type of integrated software which combines several business office functions such as a phone directory, monthly calendar, and calculator.
>sa   Time management--Computer methods--Software.

Educational games--Software.
>Assignment: Learning with Leeper, by Sierra On-Line.
>sa   Alphabet games--Software. Counting games--Software. Math games--Software. Reading games--Software.

Educational software.
>Assignment: Reading comprehension skills, by American Educational Computer.
>sa   Educational games--Software.
>sf   Computer educational games--Software.

Electronic spreadsheets--Software.
        Assignment: Multiplan, by Microsoft.

Fantasy adventure games--Software.
        Assignment: Zork II, by Infocom.
        cn   Make dual entry under COMPUTER
GAMES--SOFTWARE.

Flight--Computer simulation--Software.
        Assignment: Flight simulator, by Sub-Logic.

Household finances--Calculation--Computer methods--Software.
        Assignment: Financial cookbook, by Electronic Arts.

Integrated software.
        Assignment: Appleworks, by Apple.
        pn   Here is entered software which combines several
common applications such as word processing, database
management, and electronic spreadsheets and which enables data
to be transferred from one application to another.
        sa   Desktop management--Software.

Interactive fiction--Software.
        Assignment: Mindshadow, by Activision.
        pn   Here is entered software consisting of text or text and
graphics stories in which the player interacts with the computer
through typed commands that affect the course of the story.
        sa   Adventure games--Software.

Interactive fiction editors--Software.
        Assignment: Story tree, by Scholastic.
        pn   Here is entered software which can be used to create
interactive fiction using text or text and graphics.

Logos (Graphic design)--Computer methods--Software.
        Assignment: Print shop, by Broderbund.

Mailing labels--Production--Computer methods--Software.
        Assignment: PaperClip, by Batteries Included.

Math games--Software.
　　　　Assignment: Alligator mix, by DLM.
　　　　cn   Make dual entry under EDUCATIONAL
GAMES--SOFTWARE.

Mathematics--Computer-assisted instruction (Secondary)--Software.
　　　　Assignment: Survival math, by Sunburst Communications.

Maze puzzles--Construction--Computer methods--Software.
　　　　Assignment: Puzzles and posters, by MECC.

Menu planning--Computer methods--Software.
　　　　Assignment: The ultimate shopping machine and random
dining guide, by Solitaire.

Mystery adventure games--Software.
　　　　Assignment: Deadline, by Infocom.
　　　　cn   Make dual entry under COMPUTER
GAMES--SOFTWARE.

Nutrition--Calculation--Computer methods--Software.
　　　　Assignment: The model diet, by Softsync.

Preschoolers' software.
　　　　Assignment: Early games, by Springboard Software.
　　　　pn   Here is entered software for use by or with preschool
children.
　　　　sf   Computer software for preschoolers. Software,
Preschoolers'.

Reading games--Software.
　　　　Assignment: Elementary Prereading/counting, by MECC.
　　　　cn   Make dual entry under EDUCATIONAL
GAMES--SOFTWARE.

Recipe files--Computer methods--Software.
　　　　Assignment: The ultimate shopping machine and random
dining guide, by Solitaire.

Science fiction adventure games--Software.
　　Assignment: In search of the most amazing thing, by Spinnaker Software.
　　cn　Make dual entry under COMPUTER GAMES--SOFTWARE.

Shopping lists--Computer methods--Software.
　　Assignment: The ultimate shopping machine and random dining guide, by Solitaire.

Sports games--Software.
　　Assignment: Microsoft decathlon, by Microsoft.
　　cn　Make dual entry under COMPUTER GAMES--SOFTWARE.

Time management--Computer methods--Software.
　　Assignment: FIDO: Friend indeed organizer, by Cherry Pick Software.

Trivia games--Software.
　　Assignment: I. Q. Baseball, by Davka.
　　cn　Make dual entry under COMPUTER GAMES--SOFTWARE.

Utility software.
　　Assignment: Utility city, by Beagle Brothers.
　　sa　Epson printer--Utility software.
　　sf　Microcomputer utility software.

War games--Software.
　　Assignment: Castle Wolfenstein, by The Muse Company.
　　cn　Make dual entry under COMPUTER GAMES--SOFTWARE.

Word processing--Software.
　　Assignment: Bank Street Writer, by Broderbund.

Subdivisions

--Calculation
> Example: FOOD VALUES--CALCULATION--COMPUTER METHODS--SOFTWARE.

--Computer-assisted instruction--Software.
> cn   Use in place of STUDY AND TEACHING--SOFTWARE. May be glossed (PRIMARY), (ELEMENTARY), or (SECONDARY) if directed to a particular school grade.
> Example: SPELLING--COMPUTER-ASSISTED INSTRUCTION (ELEMENTARY)--SOFTWARE.

--Computer simulation
> cn   Use with games and educational software in which text and/or graphics realistically duplicate situations or complex relationships which can then be altered through interaction with the computer.
> Example: COMPARISON SHOPPING--COMPUTER SIMULATION--SOFTWARE.

--Construction
> Example: CROSSWORD PUZZLES--CONSTRUCTION--COMPUTER METHODS--SOFTWARE.

--Production
> Example: MAILING LABELS--PRODUCTION--COMPUTER METHODS--SOFTWARE.

RESOURCES

American Library Association. Committee on Cataloging: Description and Access. *Guidelines for Using AACR2 Chapter 9 for Cataloging Microcomputer Software.* Chicago: American Library Association, 1984.

American Library Association. Subcommittee on Subject Access to Microcomputer Software. *Guidelines on Subject Access to Microcomputer Software.* Chicago: American Library Association. To be published early 1986.

Bates, William. *The Computer Cookbook.* Garden City, NY: Quantum Press/ Doubleday, 1984/85.

Beale, Julianne. *DDC, Dewey Decimal Classification: 004-006 Data Processing and Computer Science and Changes in Related Disciplines, Revision of Edition 9.* Albany, NY: Forest Press, 1985.

Hennepin County Library. *Authority List.* 1977–. Quarterly. 42x microfiche.

Hennepin County Library Cataloging Bulletin. 1973–. Bimonthly.

InfoWorld. Popular Computing. 1979–. Weekly.

L.C. Subject Headings Weekly Lists. Washington, DC: Library of Congress, 1984–.

Microcomputer Index. Database Services. 1984–. Bimonthly.

National Education Association. *The Yellow Book.* New York: Garland, 1985.

Parent-Teacher's Microcomputing Sourcebook for Children, 1985. New York: R. R. Bowker, 1985.

Personal Computing. Hasbrouck Heights, NJ: Hayden Publications. 1983–. Monthly.

The Software Catalog: Microcomputers. New York: Elsevier, 1984–. Semi-annual.

Spanish-Language Materials: Help for the Cataloger

by Vivian M. Pisano with Curtis Lavery

Imagine yourself living abroad, in a Latin American country, for example. For quite a while you've been planning to settle there and now you've finally arrived. Your thoughts turn to learning about your new community, the services available to you, and the events and activities in which to participate, and you hope to find the latest novel by your favorite author. The local public library is where you head for information.

Having found the library (with the help of your dictionary), you enter and are reminded again that you are in a foreign environment. Neither the reference librarian nor any other public service staff member speaks your language. The catalog is of little use to you because it, too, is all in Spanish. The library collection is arranged by a classification scheme you are not familiar with and you cannot find the section to which your dictionary leads you, "Libros en Inglés." Although there are signs throughout the library, you can understand none of them. A kind reference librarian tries to help you by enunciating the words slowly and then loudly, but the words are not familiar to you.

Now imagine, or rather witness, the experience of a Spanish-speaking person using one of our public libraries. His or her predicament, however, is more acute. The tradition of American library use is not likely to be familiar, and studies have shown that the American public library plays a small part in the lives of Spanish-speaking residents.[1] This may be misconstrued by some who believe that Spanish speakers are nonreaders. But this is not so; they obtain their reading materials from other sources.[2] Cultural factors play a part in their low use of libraries and they behold the library as just another "monolithic institution."[3] Often massive and unwelcoming in appearance, the library may seem indistinguishable from other governmental agencies which have failed to meet their needs. Furthermore, the lack of sensitive bicultural and bilingual staff to whom the community can relate may contribute to their shying away.

The absence of public libraries (as we know them here) in Latin America has led to a basic unfamiliarity with what a library is and how it functions. Although bibliotecas exist, they are only subscribed to by the wealthy and educated. Librerías (bookstores), however, are plentiful. Many people do not understand that their own taxes support the library and that they can influence its administration.

During the past decade, we have seen some exemplary efforts by individual libraries to provide services for their Spanish-speaking constituencies by employing bilingual/bicultural or bilingual personnel. But the few Spanish-speaking/Hispanic librarians in our profession are most often sought for reference desk and/or outreach activities and seldom for technical services. Therefore, library tools, such as catalogs and indexes, remain undeveloped for Spanish-speaking library patrons who cannot adequately use them without assistance. Access to the Spanish-language collection becomes a difficult prospect for the Spanish-speaking patron unless a bilingual librarian is available in the library. For Spanish-speaking library patrons to effectively use the Spanish-language collection, they must be provided with bibliographic access that is intelligible to them.

Local patron access is but one consideration in providing bibliographic access to Spanish-language materials. Other considerations are shared cataloging, online accessibility, reference, interlibrary loan, and collection development.

Most of us who use online bibliographic utilities are familiar with the benefits (and drawbacks) of shared cataloging. We simplify our cataloging task by searching the bibliographic utility to locate a high quality bibliographic record that has already been cataloged by another agency. We then copy the record for our own catalog. In order for this sharing to occur, libraries follow the same cataloging standards. "High quality," then, describes those records to which the accepted standards have been applied most strictly: for description and name headings, *Anglo-American Cataloging Rules,* 2d ed.; for subject headings, *Library of Congress Subject Headings;* for classification, the Dewey or Library of Congress classification systems; for machine readable records, the MARC formats.

Complying with recognized standards for bibliographic records allows libraries to communicate with one another when accessing each other's collections. A common language facilitates reference searches and locating materials for interlibrary loan purposes. The MARC format provides us with this language. MARC fields and subfields define pieces of data within the bibliographic record whether the record itself is in English, Spanish, Chinese, or any other language. In addition, quality collection development is a benefit libraries enjoy as a result of sharing bibliographic access. A library can identify titles, specific works of an author, or subject areas to develop by searching and retrieving the information from other library files.

Libraries should derive the same benefits of bibliographic access from Spanish-language materials as they receive from English-language materials, and perhaps a little more. Shared bibliographic access, for example, becomes a more important tool for collection development when the selector is not familiar with the language or when titles published outside of the US mainstream are not easily identifiable. Including Spanish-language materials in online bibliographic utilities promotes collection activity through interlibrary loan and reference.

But how many libraries treat their Spanish-language cataloging differently from their cataloging of English materials because they cannot find "copy" online? Spanish-language collections may be given brief, nonstandard cataloging which becomes neither part of the collection they share with other libraries nor part of their own main catalogs. Or the Spanish materials will be kept with the cataloging backlog until copy is found, possibly becoming part of the permanent backlog.

Once the library provides a well-rounded collection which satisfies a variety of educational, informational, and leisure needs and interests for all segments of its community, relevant access tools should be developed. In hopes of helping as well as inspiring catalog librarians to provide for their Spanish-speaking library patrons appropriate bibliographic access to the materials meant to serve them, this article raises some issues in relation to the description and subject access of Spanish-language materials, discusses how to establish Spanish/Hispanic personal name headings, and furnishes a bibliography of reference sources and tools to use in the cataloging task.

When Spanish-speaking persons enter the public library, they should be greeted by an inviting collection with meaningful access tools. The public library should link such persons with information they need to learn about the community, available services, events and activities in which they may wish to participate, and with the novels of their choice. Satisfying the needs and interests of the Spanish-speaking community can be accomplished in several ways: we propose that one way is for technical services to provide means by which the Spanish speaker can use the library.

SPANISH PERSONAL NAMES*

In a card catalog or bibliographic file the personal name is an instrument for identification of sought-after information. Used as a main entry or subject term, the personal name is an entry to bring

---

*By Spanish personal names, we mean surnames of persons whose place of origin is a Spanish-speaking country, whether or not they reside in that country.

related works together. The degree to which a name designation for an individual can collocate information about and/or written by that individual is dependent on the conformity of the entries to a single form and choice of the name. For example, to find *Loon Lake,* one might look under Doctorow, Edgar; Edgar L.; Edgar Lawrence; E. Lawrence; or E.L. The title in question would be found—along with the author's other works, such as *Ragtime*—under E.L. at the beginning of the Doctorow, E——— section in the card catalog. Doctorow has written five novels and one play and has a very distinctive last name. In this case, the searcher's task of identifying the sought-after *Loon Lake* by Doctorow is uncomplicated.

On the other hand, if the searcher were looking for the complete works to date of Gabriel García Márquez, the search task is complicated by the choices available. Where did the cataloger place the name in the catalog? *Did* the cataloger consistently use one name form? *Did* the cataloger place the necessary references to guide the searcher to the name form used in the catalog? A given source, for example, may have listed this author's name as Gabriel García. If the cataloger chose as the entry García Márquez, Gabriel, he or she should also place the following reference to lead the searcher to that entry: García, Gabriel see García Márquez, Gabriel. This type of see reference, from the first part of a compound surname, is generally overlooked by cataloging agencies. Hispanic persons with compound last names, however, often list only the first element (father's name) of their surnames. At other times they will list the first element and the initial of the second. If no such reference exists, the searcher may utilize the browsing method to locate the author: García, Gary; García, Horacio; García, Lucia. . .on through García Bustamente, Mario; and García García, Filemón before discovering García Márquez, Gabriel. In a large library, searchers might need to leaf through 50 cards unless they conclude the search was exhausted at García, Horacio.

Standardization, both of form and choice of personal name and references, provides searchers with guidelines regarding where to look for personal names in the catalog. Standardization also assures searchers that they will find all works by and about the same individual at a single location in the file.

The catalog entry should respect both the intended user of the catalog and the individuals referenced in the file. To yield successful results, the searching experience should follow a consistent and familiar pattern for the catalog user. Moreover, the cataloger should respect the author of a work and the person about which a work is written by choosing to list the name in the catalog as the person chooses to use it and as it is used in his or her particular environment. This will consequently simplify the searcher's task by limiting the number of possible entry points.

In this country, the standard for establishing personal names is the second edition of the *Anglo-American Cataloging Rules* (*AACR2*). *AACR2* respects the author's preference and language in most cases. *AACR2*, however, focuses upon the English-speaking library user. But the cataloging focus for Spanish-language materials should be the Spanish-speaking user of a catalog in an American library. This is not to say that comprehensibility is achieved by "translating" names into Spanish. Rather, as with *AACR2* philosophy, personal names should be established as they are commonly found in works issued in the authors' language or country.

Verification of Names

The process of verification begins when the cataloger encounters a personal name in a work being cataloged for the first time by the library. Noting the place and language of publication, the cataloger analyzes the number and type of elements that the name contains. If there are multiple elements, a determination is made concerning the presence of a compound surname. One alternative for the professional who is not Spanish-speaking is to compare the names to lists of common given and surnames. If there are three or more elements, do the first two look like given names? In most cases, the last two elements will be surnames and listed as compound names.

Verification in authority sources now begins. Questions that the cataloger should keep in mind during the search are: (1) Did the individual use his or her complete name in this source? (2) Has the library cited this individual by any other variant forms? (3) What form would the end user most likely refer to? and (4) Which name form will promote consistency in the catalog? The first verification search should be completed in the library's local catalog. It is safe to search under all elements of the surname to account for misunderstood names or outdated rules. If no such surnames are found, one or more authoritative sources should be consulted.

Establishing a hierarchy of trusted sources is useful for resolving conflicts when different name forms appear, when a Library of Congress-established name form is questionable, or when there are conflicts in birth or death dates. Consistency, both within the organization and with other libraries and organizations, is the motivating factor for identifying authoritative reference sources. (A suggested list of such reference tools can be found in the Resources section that follows the text.)

Guidelines for Establishing Spanish Name Forms

The rules in Chapter 22 (Personal Names) of the *Anglo-American Cataloguing Rules,* 2d edition (*AACR2*), may be used as a guide for establishing the Spanish name, but modifications in the rules should be made if the library truly wishes to provide meaningful name headings for Spanish-language catalog records. *AACR2*'s philosophy of establishing the name form as the person prefers his or her name to be listed or how it appears in reference sources in his or her language or country is an important and necessary guiding principle for catalogers. However, the necessary Spanish-language reference sources and/or references sources published in the person's country of origin often are not regularly consulted. "Specialized" language reference sources are either not acquired by libraries or not held in the cataloging department, which may even be in a separate facility from the library proper. Thus, often only readily available English-language sources are used. If the library subscribes to a bibliographic utility, the cataloger may search other libraries' files for the name and use another library's cataloging as the authoritative source. And the larger the number of libraries using one name form, the more reason to establish that name. But what reference sources were used by the first library to establish the name form?

Spanish reference sources should be given priority over English-language works when determining name form, especially for persons whose names have been well established both in Spanish- and English-language sources. Thus, the Spanish version of Homer's Odyssey would be entered as:

Homero.
Odisea.

Appropriate cross references would link the two name forms in the catalog.

Spanish reference sources should also be used when choosing the language of the name form for persons who use more than one language and have a self-established Spanish name form. Furthermore, additions to names—like titles and descriptive phrases—should be supplied in Spanish; for instance:

Adán (Personaje bíblico)
Francisco de Asís, San

Compound surnames create special problems for catalogers. In most cases one should follow *AACR2* by entering under the first element of the compound surname, except for a married woman whose surname consists of a combination of maiden name and her husband's surname. *AACR2* prefers to enter married women whose language is Spanish and whose surname consists of a maiden paternal family name and the husband's surname under the first element of the compound surname, regardless of its nature. One should enter under the element by which the married woman bearing the compound surname prefers to be entered. As a general rule, married women whose language is English are entered under the husband's surname.

Occasionally, an author will initialize the final element of his or her surname. Again, the entry should be established as the person chooses to use his or her name. Initializing an element preceding a surname, however, is taken as an indication that the element is not used as part of the surname.

Because the author may interchangeably use his or her full compound surname or initialize the final element, or other times drop the final element altogether, it is important to provide the appropriate references for the catalog. Where LC tends to refer only from the last element of the name, Spanish names which are used in these various forms should also be referred appropriately. In most cases, Spanish compound surnames should be referred from the first element. According to a recent *Cataloging Service Bulletin,* the Library of Congress's policy is now to "make one reference under each surname element, other than particles and prefixes."[4] However, the only Spanish name example illustrating this new policy shows the following references for the established name García de Miguel, J. M. (José María):

> De Miguel, J. M. García (José María García)
> Miguel, J. M. García (José María García)
> García de Miguel, José María

No reference is shown from the single element García.

US Hispanic Name Forms

The names of Hispanic persons in the United States present a particular challenge to the cataloger. *AACR2* rules implicitly complicate the special situation of this ethnic group that resides in a predominantly English linguistic environment by instructing the cataloger to enter under the element most commonly used in the person's language or in the country of residence. A Hispanic author who writes in English and resides in the United States may choose to maintain a traditional Latin American name form. In these cases, the name should be entered as if the author were writing in Spanish.

Other US Hispanic authors may use their names in a way different from the way they would be used in this country and different from the Latin American style. Joanne del Campo lists her name as del Campo, Joanne. Again, we emphasize the importance of determining and establishing the form of name as the person wishes to use it.

A Need for Further Study

The cataloger's task in elucidating appropriate forms and choices for Spanish personal names, whether within the United States or outside it, is complicated by variant usage in names, a lack of consistency in cataloging practices, contradictions in cataloging codes, and a lack of statistical information about the use of Spanish names. Further research into the linguistic, demographic, and bibliographic dilemma surrounding the Hispanic surname is required.

Investigation to clarify library-related issues should cover the social, historical, and cultural influences on Hispanic names. Cross-cultural pressures brought to bear on individuals that influence how they maintain or change surnames should be evaluated. By cross-cultural pressures I mean those imposed upon immigrating persons who find that their surnames are being used by others in a manner different from the way they were used in the native environment. Immigration officials, for example, have been known to rearrange or misspell names on legal documents, and the immigrant becomes associated with an unfamiliar name form. Confusion over paternal and maternal surnames, incorrect spelling, and anglicization are typical situations that immigrants face. The immigration officer's error becomes the immigrant's legal name. Roberto Bendaua Arce might be documented as Arce, Roberto Bendaua. Even if his surname were correctly documented as Bendaua Arce, Roberto by the immigration officer, he still may feel further societal pressures to conform to American usage. In time, Mr. Bendaua Arce may choose to write his name as Bendaua, Roberto Arce, as if Arce were his middle name. Or his forename might be anglicized to Robert or Bob. Conforming the name to society's norm is a phenomenon particularly visible in the United States where our "melting pot" concept motivates us to accentuate conformity rather than individuality.

Specific changes in Spanish names, caused either by cross-cultural pressures or evolutionary processes, need further study. In this country, the "de" is moving away from its conjunctive purpose, now becoming part of the integral surname element. Alicia Ramos del Campo is entered as Del Campo, Alicia. And her child, Sylvia, is named Sylvia Del Campo.

The hyphenated surname is another phenomenon for study. This practice has recently been popularized in the United States among non-Hispanic women to preserve their maiden surnames, which they place as the first element of the surname. This compound name, unlike the Hispanic compound surname, is broken to allow the husband's name as the entry element; Ann Rogers marries Greg Thompson; Ann Rogers-Thompson is entered as Thompson, Ann Rogers. In Latin America and Spain, the married woman retains her name, but as the last element in the compound name and it is not broken when entered as a heading. For example, Herminia Valdes marries Edmundo Rodriguez; Herminia Valdes-Rodriguez is entered as Valdes-Rodriguez, Herminia.

Research into the placement of the maiden name within surnames, compound surnames, and hyphenated surnames, as well as the use of "de," will facilitate our understanding of the use and distribution of Hispanic names in the United States. Telephone directories, documents such as vital statistics certificates, and school enrollment records are useful tools for the researcher. Questionnaires would also be helpful for determining name use patterns in a given geographic region.

Analyzing various types of reference sources to determine patterns in treatment of names may be beneficial, too. For instance, some Latin American telephone directories ignore the second surname for filing purposes.

Fuentes, Carlos
Fuentes Obregón, Eugenia
Fuentes Brey, Miguel
Fuentes A., Nelly
Fuentes, Olegario

In this type of filing order, family members with a common paternal name are brought together. This method assists the searcher who knows only the paternal surname and forename of the person in question. Looking for characteristic usage patterns will help to build a meaningful and standardized search and retrieval system for bibliographic data.

The process of standardization when determining Spanish personal names needs further study. Absence of time and resource materials for verifying and establishing name headings force catalogers to depend on local judgment, either others' or their own. Catalogers need standardized guidelines for the task. The *Anglo-American Cataloguing Rules,* with modifications which favor the Spanish language rather than English, would provide catalogers with guidelines for establishing headings for their own local catalogs while keeping within the standards imposed by the need to communicate with other library catalogs.

In order to conduct a study of Hispanic name patterns, we must first examine the research method itself. What is a consistent and reliable technique for identifying Hispanic persons in the United States? Standard survey research methods have utilized lists of "Hispanic" names against lists of the general population to identify the target persons. But this method is biased. Many Americans of Latin American, particularly South American, origins have surnames with roots in other cultures. D'Arcangelo, Bucich, Vignaux, Pellegrini, Tollan, Abramovich, and Tonelli, for example, are Argentinian names appearing in Ernesto Sábato's *Sobre Héroes y Tumbas.* German and Italian names in Chile and Argentina, French and English names in the Caribbean, and Asian surnames in Peru and Brazil depict the heterogeneity of the Latin American populace. The "Hispanic" names list method also fails to identify female partners and children of a mixed marriage. Research techniques for elucidating the presence of Hispanics that captures these "transparent" surnames need to be developed.

SUBJECT CATALOGING

When cataloging Spanish-language materials, analyzing the subject content and assigning subject headings present the most difficulty. The first task, of identifying the concept or concepts the work represents, can best be done by a cataloger familiar with the language. A non-Spanish-speaking, but experienced cataloger, can, however, determine the contents of most Spanish-language works. The next task, determining the appropriate term or terms to describe that work, will not be as straightforward as assigning Library of Congress subject headings. Obviously, LC headings are inappropriate for describing Spanish works simply because they are in English. And even when used, LC headings do not always reflect the actual thematic content of a work nor employ terms at once familiar and relevant to persons likely to seek this literature. That's why Hennepin County Library (HCL) varied from the standard thesaurus, *Library of Congress Subject Headings,* to modify existing LC headings and create new and innovative descriptors which are more in line with current themes and usage. In the area of Hispanic topics, for example, HCL replaced the LC headings MEXICAN AMERICANS and MEXICAN AMERICAN WOMEN with CHICANOS and CHICANAS, terms which are more familiar and self-preferred.

There is wider regional and pluralistic variation in the Spanish language than there is in the English language. Dialectical, cultural, and regional differences—including those variations within the United States—direct the evolution and contribute to a phenomenon of multiple standards within one language. US Hispanics have roots throughout the Spanish-speaking world. Within this world regional terms and idiomatic phrases develop. Also, the same terms acquire different meanings. Newly arrived Hispanics speak differently from each other and from those who have been in the United States for several generations.

When developing Spanish language subject headings, factors of content, culture, form, and consistency must be considered. Terms chosen need to reflect the philosophical and cultural character of the concept, rather than merely being a literal translation of an English term. Relevant subject headings can be generated through a consistent program of community participation and resource sharing. A similar system to the one developed by HCL would work particularly well for developing Spanish subject headings. Standard sources, such as *Bilindex,* issued by the Hispanic Information Exchange (Hispanex), can be used as a springboard. Jorge Aguayo's translation of the Dewey Decimal Classification System, *Sistema de Clasificación decimal,* can also serve as an excellent source for subject headings.

DESCRIPTIVE CATALOGING

Cataloging records for works in languages other than English appear as confusing mixtures of English and the language of the work. Although the cataloger transcribes descriptive elements as the information appears in the work itself, the cataloger adds *AACR2*-prescribed English language wording or composes words and phrases in English for the descriptive elements. In the collation area, for example, English-language abbreviations and words are used for the physical description: p. (pages), v. (volumes), and leaves. The first two examples do not conflict with the Spanish language páginas and volúmenes, but "leaves" bears no resemblance to the Spanish "hojas." In the notes area, catalogers may use wording suggested by *AACR2,* compose their own phrasing, or quote directly from the work.

AACR2's instructions for providing additional descriptive information are sometimes contradictory. The cataloger is instructed to provide the English name form and abbreviations when the name of the country, state, province, etc. is to be added to the place of publication. If, however, the place of publication is unknown, yet there is a probable place of publication, the cataloger is instructed to provide the probable place in the language of the work.

Such a mixed-language cataloging record, with Spanish-language descriptive elements found in the work and English-language explanatory or *AACR2*-prescribed information, can confuse the catalog user. The question we need to ask is: for whom is the cataloging intended? If a Spanish-language work is intended for Spanish speakers, shouldn't access to that work be comprehensible to them?

But what costs are involved in providing cataloging to serve the Spanish speaker? An initial investment to create Spanish-language equivalents for standard terminology used by *AACR2* should be made. A Spanish version of *AACR1* has been issued by the Organization of American States; *AACR2* is currently being translated into Spanish by the University of Puerto Rico under the direction of María Casas de Fauce. The second cost involves adapting a "standard" record to conform to the local library's cataloging practices. Making the kinds of changes suggested here to an existing cataloging record does not jeopardize the "sharability" of that record and these changes would not affect the standard prescribed by the MARC formats for bibliographic data. The MARC formats standardize the structures of machine-readable bibliographic data by providing standard content designators for individual data elements. Describing the data elements in the Spanish language alters neither the content designators, i.e., field tags and subfields, nor the meaning of information contained within the designation.

To serve bilingual populations, Canadian libraries vary cataloging practices according to their local needs. The National Library of Canada offers true bilingual cataloging by providing two separate cataloging records—one in English and the other in French. N. K. Jain studied the cataloging practices of libraries in the province of Quebec and found that most libraries did not issue two separate records but tended to prefer the language of the work for entering descriptive elements. Bilingual works were given two separate cataloging records. *AACR2,* both the English version and a French translation, serves as the standard for most of the libraries studied.[5]

Special Considerations

Whether or not the cataloger tailors the cataloging record for the Spanish-speaking user, the cataloger should consider Spanish-language conventions and Spanish book publishing peculiarities when making descriptive cataloging decisions.

Initial articles should be disregarded for filing purposes. These articles are el, la, los, las, un(o), una, unos, and unas. (However, when these words function as pronouns and appear in the initial position, they *should* dictate filing order.) Also to be disregarded in filing are initial inverted question and exclamation marks, which usually do not appear as part of the character set of typewriters, computer keyboards, and output devices anyway.

Diacritical marks used in the Spanish language are the acute accent (ŕ) and the umlaut (··). (The umlaut is used over the letter "u" when that letter is pronounced in the "gu" construction.) Accent marks are often omitted from capitalized letters. The cataloger should be aware of their presence when transcribing a capitalized title, phrase, or name to upper and lower case.

Publication dates, printing dates, and edition statements of Spanish-language materials create the most confusion for catalogers. "Edición" does not necessarily translate directly to the English meaning of "edition"; it often indicates a subsequent printing. Printing "ediciones" and their associated dates do not appear on the title page but most often on the verso of the title page. A method one might follow is to use the copyright date as a guideline. If the copyright date is followed by one or more subsequent "ediciones" use only the copyright date. If an "edición" is copyrighted or it has been revised and/or amplified, consider it to be a different edition. Use the publication date in conjunction with the copyright date if the date of publication appears on the title page.

Spanish-language books are often issued as part of a publisher series and frequently as part of a subseries. If the library's policy is to trace publisher series, the cataloger should take care when determining whether the series under consideration is part of a larger series.

Cataloging for Spanish-speaking patrons is a feasible task for those libraries concerned with providing appropriate and meaningful service to their communities. The issues discussed here regarding personal names, subject cataloging, and descriptive cataloging are not by any means intended as a comprehensive coverage of cataloging Spanish-language materials but rather as an attempt to provide some guidelines and considerations for catalogers who are knowledgeable about cataloging English-language items but feel uncertain about Spanish-language works.

Providing meaningful bibliographic access for Spanish-speaking persons is an important but often overlooked means of encouraging library use. If your first library experience in a country where you chose to live and where you pay taxes was similar to that of a Spanish-speaking person's experience in an American library, would you return? Would you encourage your family and friends to visit the library?

Imagine that the library were aware of the significant size of its English-speaking community and made efforts to serve your community. You might find a catalog that you could use to access the English-language collection. This catalog would perhaps arrange the entries under English-language subject headings, follow familiar filing conventions, reflect how American surnames are used and entered, and contain additional entries for second editions. It is likely that you would visit the library more than once and encourage others to do so too. You might even be inspired to become a more active participant in library services by assisting with the development and refinement of bibliographic tools that would be more responsive to your community's needs.

REFERENCES

1. Pisano, Vivian M., and Margaret Skidmore. *A Study of Library Use within a Spanish Speaking Community.* (unpublished). Richmond, CA, 1977, p. 30.
2. Guernica, Antonio, and Irene Kasperuk. *Reaching the Hispanic Market Effectively* (New York: McGraw-Hill, 1982). (Also, Pisano & Skidmore, p. 30.)
3. Pisano & Skidmore, p. 33.
4. *Cataloging Service Bulletin* 27 (Winter 1985), p. 33.
5. Jain, N. K. "Serving the Bilingual Client; a Problem in Catalogue Access in the Province of Quebec." *Ontario Library Review* 65 (3) (September 1981), p. 183–86.

RESOURCES

General

Diccionario enciclopédico Espasa. 8. ed. Madrid: Espasa-Calpe, 1978. 12 vols.

Diccionario enciclopédico Salvat universal. Barcelona: Salvat, 1970.

Diccionario enciclopédico U.T.E.&H.A. México: Unión Tipogrráfica Editorial Hispano-Americana, 1950–52.

Personal Names

Flores, Angel. *Bibliografía de escritores hispanoamericanos—A bibliography of Spanish American Writers, 1609–1974.* New York: Gordian Press, 1975. 318 pages.

Foster, David William (comp.) *A Dictionary of Contemporary Latin American Authors.* Tempe, AZ: Arizona State Univertsity, 1975. 110 pages.

Handbook of Latin American Studies. No. 1– 1935–. Gainesville, FL: University of Florida Press. Annual.

Kay, Ernest (ed.) *Dictionary of Latin and Caribbean Biography.* London: Melrose Press, 1971. 459 pages.

Lorona, Lionel V. *Bibliography of Latin American Bibliographies, 1982–1983.* Madison, WI: Salalm, 1984. 33 pages.

Palau y Dulcet, Antonio. *Manual del librero hispanoamericano; bibliografía general espauola e hispanoamericana desde la invención de la imprenta hasta nuestros tiempos.* Barcelona: A. Palau. 1948–. 28 vols.

Reglas de catalogación anglo-americanas, texto norteamericano. Washington, DC: Secretaría General de la Organización de Estados Americanos, 1970.

Valk, Barbara G. (comp.) *HAPI Thesaurus and Name Authority, 1975–1977.* Los Angeles: University of California, Los Angeles, 1979. 113 pages.

Woods, Richard D. *Hispanic First Names.* Westport, CT: Greenwood Press, 1984. 224 pages.

Geographic Names

Atlas geográfica ilustrada de nuestro mundo. Barcelona: Sopena, 1984.

Atlas universal Aguilar. Madrid: Aguilar, 1954.

International Federation of Library Associations and Institutions. *Names of States: An Authority List of Language Forms for Catalogue Entries.* London: IFLA International Office for UBC, 1981.

Subject Heading Sources

Bilindex: A Bilingual Spanish-English Subject Heading List. Oakland, CA: Hispanex, 1984. 533 pages.

Chicano Periodical Index: A Cumulative Index to Selected Periodicals. Boston: G. K. Hall, 1983.

Sistema de clasificación decimal. Albany, NY: Forest Press, 1980. 3 vols.

Valk, Barbara G., ed. *Hispanic American Periodicals Index, 1970–74.* Los Angeles: University of California, Los Angeles, 1984.

Cataloging Comics

by Randall Scott

The idea of deliberately collecting comic books and other comics material for a permanent collection in an academic library dates back to about 1970. At the beginning of 1985, there were 35 libraries with permanent comics collections, according to the *Fandom Directory*.[1] Research libraries have devoted large amounts of expensive storage space to comic books with the expectation that these collections will prove to be resources for cultural investigation. Now that these collections are becoming well established, research librarians are beginning to consider the possibility of cataloging comic books.

Comic book collections in public and school libraries differ in character from those in research libraries. Some public and school libraries have been offering comic books to their users since at least the 1970s, but they are sometimes valued less for their content than for their power to attract customers. Comic books have been used to entice non-users into the building for purposes other than reading comics (i.e., to trick them into reading "real" books). Some public libraries trade with users rather than keeping and loaning specific comic books, so that the collection has a rotating stock.[2] In these libraries, formal cataloging has not been a realistic possibility, because the collections change rapidly either through trading or deterioration.

It is discouraging to find that for the past 50 years, when American comic book companies have been building up a phenomenal publishing record (at least 5,000 titles), American research libraries have done almost nothing to record the medium bibliographically. But cataloging of comic books will have to be done before large collections can be used efficiently. The universe of comics is so large that serious research can scarcely be expected to flourish until it is possible to gauge the completeness and extent of a given collection in some detail. To date, only the Michigan State University (MSU) Libraries' collection of over 30,000 comic art items is being systematically cataloged. Insights, practices, and examples derived from experience with the MSU collection follow.

BOOKS OF COMIC STRIPS

Bibliographically speaking, comics are a little more complicated than most entertainment media. The naturally occuring "unit" of publication is the comic strip, which is not published by itself but appears inside some other bibliographic entity: a newspaper, book, or magazine. Of these three common formats, only the book form has any history of cataloging by libraries.

Comic strips published in books are usually reprint collections from newspaper or magazine comics. A typical book collection will display a strip title either as the title of the book or as a series title. Occasionally the strip title is less prominent, but it should still be traced by the cataloger when known. The Library of Congress has given instructions to this effect.

> When cataloging an item that is about or consists of selections from a comic strip, single panel cartoon, etc., make an added entry for the title of the comic strip, etc., if this title does not also begin the title proper for the item being cataloged. If necessary, justify the added entry by a note.

> Trudeau, G. B., 1948–
>   [Doonesbury. Selections]
>   Stalking the perfect tan ...

>   I.Title. II. Title: Doonesbury.[3]

This instruction is equally important for the relatively new "graphic novel" format. Even though the material may be original and not reprinted from a newspaper strip, it will often have a strip title as well as a book and/or episode titles. Aside from this, and a later recommendation to add subject headings where appropriate, the book format should present few cataloging novelties.

THE COMIC BOOK FORMAT

Some research libraries are beginning to catalog comic books, best described as "magazines devoted to the publication of comic strips." The overwhelming majority of comic books are serials which are published regularly in monthly, bimonthly, or quarterly cycles. However, until 1979, comic books were not admitted into the national serials database *New Serial Titles.*[4] No library in the United States had cataloged more than a handful of titles before 1980.

Luckily, there are two excellent sourcebooks for comic book cataloging information. Although *The Comic Book Price Guide* and *The Official Underground and Newave Comix Price Guide*[5] both proclaim themselves to be "price guides," it is the publishing information they provide that is vital for cataloging accuracy and completeness. Both are reliable guides for dates of first and last issues and title changes, and both should be consulted whenever cataloging a US comic book.

Deciding what the title of a comic book "really" is can be as difficult for the cataloger as it often is for the new comic book collector. The convention in the comics industry is to keep the indicia or masthead title constant and to allow the editor some flexibility with the cover title. Once this is known, the collector will have little difficulty identifying even very complex titles. This publishers' practice is explained at the beginning of the alphabetical listing in each year's *Comic Book Price Guide*. Unfortunately for comic book catalogers, the *Anglo-American Cataloguing Rules*, 2nd ed., specify that the cover title is to be preferred as a source of information over the masthead title.[6] Considerable common sense and flexibility are required of the cataloger to avoid creating silly and unnecessary title changes where none may have occurred. The only rule that can sensibly apply is this: Always trace the masthead title (the part conventionally printed in all capital letters) if you are cataloging from the cover. A second rule should probably remain unwritten but here it is: Always look for excuses to enter comic books under the masthead title, because the *AACR2* way of doing it is just plain wrong.

VERTICAL FILES OF COMIC STRIP CLIPPINGS

Newspaper comic strips have apparently never been accorded entries when cataloging newspapers. It is convenient, however, to collect clipped comic strips in vertical files and to catalog those files. The files can also include clippings about a given comic strip and thus be locally assembled information resources on subjects for which no books have been written. This is particularly important in a new field like comics, because there are so many topics on which no books have been written, but any permanent vertical file can be treated in this way.

The OCLC MARC format allows libraries to create records with the designation "bib lvl c," which can be translated to mean "a locally assembled collection, not a published work." Here are some samples from the MSU catalog.[7]

SpecColl
       Sports comics : clipping file. -- [19
PCVF   --]-
COMICS   1 portfolio ; 25 x 38 cm.
       Collected at Michigan State
University in the Russel B. Nye Popular
Culture Collection's Popular Culture
Vertical File (PCVF).

      1. Sports comics--History and
criticism I. Russel B. Nye Popular
Culture Collection

MiEM   29 NOV 84   11431569   EEMJme

SpecColl
      Women characters in comics : clipping
PCVF   file. -- [19--]-
COMICS   1 portfolio ; 25 x 38 cm.
       Collected at Michigan State
University in the Russel B. Nye Popular
Culture Collection's Popular Culture
Vertical File (PCVF).

      1. Women in popular culture
2. Superheroine comics--History and
criticism 3. Women in art 4. Women in
literature I. Russel B. Nye Popular
Culture Collection

MiEM   29 NOV 84   11433812   EEMJme

SpecColl
        Underground comics : clipping file. --
PCVF   [196-]-
COMICS   1 portfolio ; 25 x 38 cm.
        Collected at Michigan State
University in the Russel B. Nye Popular
Culture Collection's Popular Culture
Vertical File (PCVF).

        1. Underground comics--History and
criticism I. Russel B. Nye Popular
Culture Collection

MiEM   29 NOV 84   11431640   EEMJme

SpecColl
        Mosley, Zack.
PCVF   Zack Mosley : clipping file. -- [19
COMICS --]-
        1 portfolio ; 25 x 38 cm.
        Collected at Michigan State
University in the Russel B. Nye Popular
Culture Collection's Popular Culture
Vertical File (PCVF).
        Includes material on Smilin' Jack.

        1. Mosley, Zack. 2. Aeronautics--
Comic books, strips, etc.--History and
criticism I. Russel B. Nye Popular
Culture Collection II. Smilin' Jack
III. Title

MiEM   29 NOV 84   11433721   EEMJme

CLASSIFICATION

The Library of Congress classification schedule for comics, slightly abbreviated, appears below.

Comic Books, Strips, Etc.[8]

PN 6700 Periodicals, societies, etc.
    6702 Congresses
    6705 Exhibitions, museums, etc.
    6707 Encyclopedias. Dictionaries
    6710 General works including history
    6712 Moral and religious aspects
    6714 Other special topics
    6720 General collections
         By region or country:
6725–6728 United States
6735–6738 Great Britain
6745–6748 France
6755–6758 Germany
6765–6768 Italy
6775–6778 Spain
    6790 Other regions or countries, A-Z

The system divides the four numbers for each country as follows: (1) History; (2) Collections; (3) Individual authors or works; (4) Individual comic strips, by title.

The application of this system presents some difficulties. What do you do with a book that collects and criticizes the Donald Duck strips by Carl Barks? It could be argued into any of the four categories. Most books that reprint comics appear to fit in any of the three latter catagories, because they are collecting material from various places of original publication and because they typically focus on a single writer, a single artist, and a single strip.

What do you do with the comic book *Walt Disney's Comics and Stories* (*WDC&S*) which has published dozens of different strips (by dozens of different writers and artists) that cover more than 40 years? *WDC&S* is a perfectly typical comic book, but it appears to be left out of the Library of Congress scheme. The second category, "collections," is normally used for reprint books and serials that collect more than one strip title, whether from comic books or newspaper strips. Some comic books could fit here, but most comic books are not collections in this sense. The third category, "individual authors or works," is usually used for books about single writers or artists and for collections of their works that go beyond reprinting a single strip title. A comic book is rarely the work of an individual, although there are some cases in which a comic book might be classified here.

The fourth category, "individual comic strips, by title," catches most of the reprint collections of newspaper comic strips, since they are typically edited by collecting a single strip. This fourth category is probably the most nearly logical place to put comic books, although they would have to be entered by comic book title and not by strip title. This works well for small collections and can be used especially for countries that do not publish very many comic books. It would be best to add a fifth category specifically for comic books, and indeed the way the schedule is constructed it would be possible for the Library of Congress to add one someday. The solution to the problem adopted by Michigan State University Libraries is described in Exhibit 1.

SUBJECT HEADINGS

The heading COMIC BOOKS, STRIPS, ETC. is the central Library of Congress term for comics material. It can be used both as a primary heading and as a free-floating subhead. The MSU practice is to apply the heading, alone and with geographical subdivisions, to anthologies. Works about comics are given the subheading HISTORY AND CRITICISM or other appropriate subheadings. The Library of Congress uses the subheading HISTORY AND CRITICISM part of the time and does not apply the subheading COMIC BOOKS, STRIPS, ETC. to anthologies. The result is inconsistent and serves to minimize the number of items found in the subject catalog.

In its *Subject Cataloging Manual* (1984), the Library of Congress spelled out a policy of not using the subdivision COMIC BOOKS, STRIPS, ETC. under individual literary authors. Catalogers are instructed to use the phrase [AUTHORS NAME] IN FICTION, DRAMA, POETRY, ETC. instead.[9] The disadvantage of this practice is that it conceals the comics format by lumping it in with fiction, drama, and poetry, not even preserving the word "comics" in the subject listing. In libraries that particularly wish to emphasize the comics format to their users (and this probably includes many public libraries and all serious special collections), this LC instruction should probably not be followed. (Actually, a comic book about a literary author is rarely seen. The matter is mentioned here to show the level of recognition currently given to comics by the Library of Congress: comics are just important enough to be given a cross-reference telling us not to use the term! The idea that comics might be a unique and important literary/artistic medium is only very slowly penetrating the nation's most conservative subject thesaurus.)

The most important distinctions in subject matter among comics themselves are spelled out in the generic labels that most comic books carry. The genre designations (such as "western") are just as informative to the prospective reader as the word "chemistry" on a chemistry book. The Library of Congress has allowed one generic heading to be born (WESTERN COMIC BOOKS, STRIPS, ETC.), but otherwise no such distinctions are acknowledged. Using the genre names for subject headings is a natural and useful way to help the library user find preferred kinds of comics. The most common genres (and the recommended headings) are ROMANCE COMICS, SUPERHERO COMICS, WESTERN COMICS, WAR COMICS, UNDERGROUND COMICS, SCIENCE FICTION COMICS, FANTASY COMICS, DETECTIVE AND MYSTERY COMICS, FUNNY ANIMAL COMICS, FUNNY KID COMICS, and TEEN HUMOR COMICS. These headings fit in nicely with existing Library of Congress headings that describe other kinds of storytelling. A complete list of the headings used in cataloging comics at MSU can be found in Exhibit 2, and several samples of MSU records appear in Exhibit 3.

EXHIBIT 1
Modifications to the Library of Congress Comic Book Schedule as Used by the Michigan State University Libraries

The MSU call number system differs from the LC schedule only in its treatment of US comic books. Grouping is by the decade in which a serial begins, with subgrouping by publisher. With this system, the shelflist becomes a tool for chronological studies as well as a publisher index to the collection. Items in the classifications PN 6728.1 through PN 6728.5 are restricted by size to the normal comic book dimensions of 26 or 28 cm., and thus shelving of this massive collection can be done with uniform shelf spacing. Odd-sized comics, e.g. tabloids, digests, and Big Little Books, are grouped in the LC class number PN 6728 by inserting a publisher cutter.

PN 6728   Individual comic strips or comic books, by title, A–Z. Use for early comic books (before 1935) and comic books in unusual formats, e.g., Big Little Books and tabloids. If useful to group unusual formats on shelf, cutter by publisher, then by entry. Publisher cutters in use:

.A385   Alcoholics Anonymous
.C29   Campus Crusade for Christ

.C47 Chick Publications (Jack T. Chick)
.M378 Marvel Comics Group (tabloids)
.M6   Modern Promotions
.N333 National/DC Comics (tabloids & digests)
.W47 Whitman and Western (Big Little Books & digests)
.W6   World Syndicate

PN 6728.1 Golden Age comic books, titles beginning between 1935 and 1949, by publisher, A–Z, then by title. Publisher cutters in use:

.A2   Ace/A.A. Wynn
.A5   American Comics Group (ACG)
.A7   Archie
.A85   Avon
.C6   Columbia
       DC: see National
.D4   Dell
.E5   Enwil
.F3   Fawcett
.F5   Fiction House
.F6   Fox Features
.G5   Gilberton
.G55   Lev Gleason
.H3   Harvey
.H5   Hillman
       MLJ: see Archie
.M25   D. McKay
.M27   Magazine Enterprises
.M3   Timely/Marvel
.M4   Melverne
.N3   National
.N4   Nedor
.N6   Novelty
.P3   Parents Magazine
.P7   Prize
.Q3   Quality
.S75   Street & Smith
       Timely: see Marvel
.U5   United Features
       Wynn, A.A.: see Ace

PN 6728.2 Fifties comic books, titles beginning from 1950 to 1959, by publisher, then by title. Publisher cutters in use:

.A7   Archie/Radio

	Atlas: see Marvel
.C47	Charlton
.D4	Dell
.E14	E.C.
.F3	Fawcett
.G4	General Electric Company
.G5	Gilberton
.H33	Harvey
.M25	Magazine Enterprises
.M3	Marvel/Atlas
.N3	National
	Radio: see Archie
.Q3	Quality
.Z5	Ziff-Davis

PN 6728.3 Silver Age comic books, titles beginning from 1960 to 1969, by publisher, A–Z, then by title. Publisher cutters in use:

.A7	Archie/Radio
	DC: see National
.C47	Charlton
.E32	Eerie Publications
.G56	Gold Key
.G6	B.F. Goodrich
.H3	Harvey
.M3	Marvel
.N3	National
	Radio: see Archie
.T6	Tower
.U5	U.S. Government
.W3	Warren

PN 6728.4 Seventies comic books, titles beginning from 1970 to 1979, by publisher, A–Z, then by title. Publisher cutters in use:

.A7	Archie
.A8	Atlas
	DC: see National
.C47	Charlton
.C48	Chick Publications
	Disney: see Walt Disney
.E32	Eerie Publications
.G56	Gold Key/Western
.H3	Harvey
.M3	Marvel
.N3	National

.O5   Omnibus
.R3   Radio Shack
.R4   Fleming H. Revell
.S75   Star*Reach
.W3   Walt Disney Productions
.W33   Warren
         Western: see Gold Key
.W6   Word Books

PN 6718.45 Underground comic books, titles beginning from about 1967, by publisher, A–Z, then by title. Publisher cutters in use:

.A2   Publisher unknown
.A6   Adam's Apple
.A6   Apex Novelties
.C3   California Grimpet
.C35   Cartoonists Co-op
.C6   Company and Sons
.D7   Dragon Seed
.E25   Ecomix
.E3   Educomix
.E87   Everyman
.F7   Fragments West
.G7   Warren Greenwood
.H5   C.P. Himes
.K3   Karma Komix
.K5   Kitchen Sink/Krupp
.L3   Last Gasp
.L5   Limestone Press
.N3   Nanny Goat
.N6   N.A.C.L.A.
.P4   Harvey Pekar
.P7   Print Mint
.Q3   Sal Quartuccio
.R4   Recycled Reality
.R5   Rip Off Press
.S3   San Francisco Comic Book Co.
.S5   Siegel & Simon
.S75   Stampart
.Y3   Yahoo
.Y4   Yentzer & Gonif

PN 6728.5 Eighties comic books, titles beginning from 1980 to 1989, by publisher, A–Z, then by title. Publisher cutters in use:

.A7	Archie
.C47	Charlton
.C6	Comico
.D3	DC
.E25	Eclipse
.E3	Educomics
.F3	Fantaco
.F5	First
.M3	Marvel
	National: see DC
.N4	New Media
.P3	Pacific
.R4	Fleming H. Revell
.W47	Western

PN 6728.55 New wave comix, minis, other amateur and self-published stripzines, titles beginning about 1980, by publisher or creator, A–Z, then by title. Publisher cutters in use:

.B6	Jacques Boivin
.C6	Comix World
.D5	Clark A. Dissmeyer
.H6	Matt Howarth
.J3	Jabberwocky Graphix
.M3	Rick McCollum
.P47	Phantasy Press
.R9	J. Ryan
.S5	Jim Siergey
.W45	Steve Willis

EXHIBIT 2
Local Subject Headings for Comics Material as Used by the Michigan State University Libraries

These headings are applied to both monographic and serial comics items. Works about the various genres receive the subheading HISTORY AND CRITICISM. Of the headings listed here, only WESTERN COMIC BOOKS, STRIPS, ETC. is used by the Library of Congress.

Adventure story comics
    xx Comic books, strips, etc.
    sa Prehistoric adventure comics
        Jungle adventure comics

Afro-American comics
    xx Comic books, strips, etc.--United States

Career girl comics
    xx Comic books, strips, etc.

Comic books, strips, etc.--Publication and distribution
    xx Publishers and publishing

Detective and mystery comics
    x Mystery comics
      Crime comics
      Detective comics
      Crime and criminals--comic books, strips, etc.
      Detectives--Comic books, strips, etc.
    xx Comic books, strips, etc.

Fantasy comics
    xx Comic books, strips, etc.
    sa Sword and sorcery comics

Funny animal comics
    xx Comic books, strips, etc.
        Animals--Caricatures and cartoons

Funny ghost comics
    xx Comic books, strips, etc.
        Funny horror comics

Funny horror comics
    xx Comic books, strips, etc.
        Horror comics
    sa Funny ghost comics

Funny kid comics
    xx Comic books, strips, etc.
    sa Rich kid comics

Funny war comics

      x Military comics
         Funny soldier comics
     xx Comic books, strips, etc.
         War comics
     sa War comics

Girls' comics
     xx Comic books, strips, etc.

Gothic romance comics
      x Love comics
     xx Comic books, strips, etc.
         Horror comics
         Romance comics

Horror comics
     xx Comic books, strips, etc.
     sa Gothic romance comics
         Funny horror comics

Jungle adventure comics
     xx Comic books, strips, etc.
         Adventure story comics

Kung fu comics
      x Martial arts--Comic books, strips, etc.
     xx Comic books, strips, etc.

New Wave Comics
      x Nuwave comics
     xx Comic books, strips, etc.
         Underground comics

Newspapers--Sections, columns, etc.--Comics
      x Newspaper comics
     xx Comic books, strips, etc.

Prehistoric adventure comics
      x Caveman comics
     xx Comic books, strips, etc.
         Adventure story comics

Romance comics
      x Love comics

> xx Comic books, strips, etc.
> sa Gothic romance comics

Science fiction comics
> xx Comic books, strips, etc.

Sports comics
> xx Comic books, strips, etc.
> Sports--Comic books, strips, etc.

Spy Comics
> x Espionage--Comic books, strips, etc.
> Spies--Comic books, strips, etc.
> xx Comic books, strips, etc.

Superhero comics
> xx Comic books, strips, etc.

Superheroes in fiction
> xx Comic books, strips, etc.

Superheroine comics
> xx Comic books, strips, etc.
> Women's comics
> sa Women's comics

Sword and sorcery comics
> xx Comic books, strips, etc.
> Fantasy comics

Teen humor comics
> xx Comic books, strips, etc.

Underground comics
> x Head comics
> x Comix
> xx Comic books, strips, etc.
> Underground press
> sa New wave comics

War comics
> x War--Comic books, strips, etc.
> Military comics
> xx Comics books, strips, etc.

Funny war comics
    sa Funny war comics

Western comic books, strips, etc.
    x Cowboys--Comic books, strips, etc.
    xx Comic books, strips, etc.

Women's comics
    x Feminism--Comic books, strips, etc.
    xx Comic books, strips, etc.
        Superheroine comics
    sa Superheroine comics

EXHIBIT 3
Sample Records from the Catalog of the Comic Art Collection at the Michigan State University Libraries

```
SpecColl
            Mills, Pat
PN              The A.B.C. warriors. Book 1 / by Pat
6738        Mills, Kevin O'Neill and Mike McMahon.
.A2         -- London, England : Titan Books, 1983.
M5              79 p. : ill. ; 28 cm.
1983            ISBN 0-907610-11-0


            1. Science fiction comics 2. War
        comics I. O'Neill, Kevin II. McMahon,
        Mike III. Title IV. Title: The ABC
        warriors


MiEM     12 DEC 84     11483622     EEMJme


SpecColl
            Fantastic four. New York, Marvel Comics
PN          Group.
6728.3                  v. col. ill. 26 cm.
.M3         Began with no. 1 (November 1961)
F3          All issues also called v.1.
            Key title: Fantastic four, ISSN 0274-5291


            1. Superhero comics


MiEM     31 AUG 81     6387681     EEMRme     SN80-12850
```

```
SpecColl
            The history of natural gas / prepared
PN             by the Educational Service Bureau,
6728.3         American Gas Association. -- New
.A53           York, N.Y. : American Gas
H5             Association, 1960.
1960           15 p. : col. ill. ; 26 cm.
               Cover title.



            1. Gas, Natural--Comic books, strips,
         etc. I. American Gas Association

MiEM     07 DEC 84     11465037      EEMJme
```

```
SpecColl
            Hot Rod King. -- Chicago, Ill. :
PN             Approved Comics, 1952.
6728.2         1 v. : col. ill. ; 26 cm.
.Z5            Bimonthly.
H6             No. 1 (Fall [1952]).
               Ziff-Davis comic group
               Title from cover.



            1. Sports comics 2. Automobile
         racing--Comic books, strips, etc.

MiEM     07 DEC 84     11463594      EEMJme
```

SpecColl
       Mason, Brenda D.
GV   George Foster : man of dreams, man
865   with a purpose / [written by Brenda D.
.F62   Mason ; story layout and character art
M3   by Morrie Turner ; lettering and color
1982   by Ray Salmon]. -- [Tempe, Az.] :
George Foster Enterprises, 1982.
    [16] p. : col. ill. ; 26 cm.
    Title from cover.
    Caption title: George Foster, a dream
comes true.
    Received through CAPA-alpha.
    1. Foster, George, 1948 Dec. 1---
Comic books, strips, etc. 2. Baseball
players--Biography--Comic books,
strips, etc. 3. Sports comics
I. Turner, Morrie II. Title

MiEM   12 DEC 84   11483588   EEMJme

SpecColl
       Shelton, Gilbert.
PN   Six snappy sockeroos from the
6728.45 archives of the fabulous furry freak
.R5   brothers and Fat Freddy's cat / Gilbert
F26   Shelton. -- San Francisco, CA : Rip Off
1980   Press, 1980.
    [48] p. : ill. ; 26 cm. -- (Fabulous
furry freak brothers ; no. 6)
    Title from cover.

    1. Underground comics 2. Funny
animal comics I. Title II. Title: Fat
Freddy's cat III. Series

MiEM   07 DEC 84   11465123   EEMJme

```
SpecColl
           Tarzān wa-La`nat al-Af`ā. -- [Cairo] :
PN         Matba'at al-Ma'rifah, [1978?].
6790       17 p. : ill. ; 24 cm.
.E344      Title from cover.
T3         In the Arabic alphabet.
1978       Tarzan comics translated to Arabic.



           1. Jungle adventure comics
         I. Tarzan. Arabic


MiEM     12 DEC 84     11482511     EEMJme




SpecColl
           Wonder Woman. -- New York : Wonder
PN         Woman Pub. Co.,
6728.1        v. : col. ill. ; 26 cm.
.N3        Quarterly, Monthly.
W6         Began with no. 1 (Summer 1942)
           Title from cover.
           Description based on no. 6 (Fall
           1943)



           1. Superheroine comics


MiEM     30 SEP 81     7804088     EEMRme
```

REFERENCES

1. "Research Libraries of Interest to Fandom," (in *Fandom Directory,* 1985–1986 ed., San Bernardino, CA: Fandom Computer Services, 1985, p. 57–62). Libraries reporting special collections of comics material are:

Boston University: 44 years of original Little Orphan Annie art.

Bowling Green State University (Ohio): 20,000 comic books.

California State University, Fullerton: 2,000 comic books.

College de Sherbrooke (Quebec): 5,000 European comics items.

Comic Research Library (Tappen, British Columbia): 200,000 newspaper strips, 1,000 comic books.

Comics Magazine Association of America (New York City): 2,000 comic books.

Fairleigh Dickinson University (Madison, New Jersey): 4,000 pieces of original comic art.

Indiana University Lilly Library: extensive Marvel comics.

Iowa State University: 1,500 underground comics, 84 EC comics.

Kent State University (Ohio): 125 comic books, some original cartoon art.

Library of Congress: 45,000 comic books.

Michigan State University: 30,000 comic books.

Murdoch University (Western Australia): sample comic books.

Museum of Cartoon Art (Portchester, New York): 60,000 pieces of original comics and cartoon art.

Northwestern University (Illinois): 8,500 comic books, 100 Big Little Books.

Ohio Historical Society: comics in Zane Grey collection.

Ohio State University: extensive original art, growing collection of comic books.

San Francisco Academy of Comic Art: 4,500,000 newspaper strips, several thousand comic books.

Southern Illinois University, Edwardsville: 1,500 comic books.

State Historical Society of Wisconsin: extensive comic books.

Syracuse University: samples of cartoon art and comic strips.

University of California, Los Angeles: extensive comic books.

University of Chicago: 45 boxes of comic books.

University of Connecticut: 150 underground comics.

University of Kansas: original cartoon art of 600 cartoonists, 500 Big Little Books.

University of Kentucky: some comics.

University of Maryland: 1,000 comic books.

University of Minnesota: 1,200 comic books, 500 Little Big Books.

University of New Brunswick: some comics.

University of Oregon: comic books in Gardner Fox collection.

University of Pittsburgh: 8,500 comic books.

University of Sydney (Australia): 12,000 comic books.

University of Virginia: some original comic strip art.

Virginia Commonwealth University: Billy De Beck (Barney Google) collection.

Washington State University: extensive underground and new wave comix.

2. *The U*N*A*B*A*S*H*E*D Librarian* 15 (Spring 1975): 4; 18 (Winter 1976): 3. Short articles describing the use of comic books in public library branches.

3. Library of Congress *Cataloging Service Bulletin* 27 (Winter 1985): 24.

4. *Comic Art Collection* 4 (November 1979); 5 (February 1980). Newsletter of the Russel B. Nye Popular Culture Collection at Michigan State University Library.

5. Overstreet, Robert M. *The Comic Book Price Guide.* Annual. Cleveland, TN: Overstreet Publications; distributed by Harmony Books, New York, and Kennedy, Jay. *The Official Underground and Newave Comix Price Guide.* Cambridge, MA: Boatner Norton Press, 1982; distributed by Crown Publishers.

6. *Anglo-American Cataloguing Rules,* 2d ed. (Chicago: American Library Association, 1978): 249.

7. *Online Systems Books Format.* (Dublin, OH: OCLC, 1984): FF-3: Bibliographic Level code "c" applies to collections arbitrarily formed by the cataloging or inputting library, when the cataloging library does not consider the individual items significant enough to warrant separate cataloging.

8. *Library of Congress Classification, Class P, Subclasses PN, PR, PS, PZ,* 2d ed. (Washington, DC: Library of Congress: 1978): 88–89.

9. *Subject Cataloging Manual: Subject Headings.* Preliminary ed. (Washington DC: Library of Congress, 1984): H1155.4/6. This manual includes a section called "Comics and comic characters" (p. H1430/1-2) which addresses only books about comics.

Cataloging Children's Materials: A Stage of Transition.

by Florence E. DeHart and Marylouise D. Meder

Just as children, defined here as through junior-high level, go through stages, so does the cataloging of children's material. Although we do not attempt to identify discrete historical stages, we hypothesize that children's cataloging now approaches a transition stage. To date, the profession's attempts at improving practices in the area of children's cataloging have failed to identify and explain the theory and knowledge base behind practice. This base includes such areas as (1) the objectives of children's cataloging and catalogs, (2) the relation of children's cataloging to adult cataloging, (3) the standardization of children's cataloging, and (4) the relation of children's cataloging to other library functions. We predict that the study of children's use of online public access computerized catalogs will serve as a catalyst to a new stage characterized by the development of a theoretical rationale.

Although public access catalogs are not a panacea for children's cataloging problems, they do offer certain qualitative approaches to organization and access beyond those that card catalogs afford. A particular advantage is the potential for evaluating retrieval output in relation to the interaction among search statements, search strategies, and the format and content of bibliographic records. Ongoing study within the context of needed broader research on how children seek, process, and use library materials and information could lead to the development of relevant hypotheses and finally to a knowledge and theory base for cataloging children's materials. After presenting historical background, this essay analyzes gaps in the four above-mentioned theory and knowledge base areas and shows how the study of children's use of online public access catalogs could help close them.

HISTORICAL BACKGROUND

The importance of children's cataloging reflects the value librarians place on children's literature, children's services, and children themselves. Providing special reading and instructional materials for children has concerned adults for centuries. During medieval times, monks copied a few manuscripts designed for children's use. After the invention of printing in the fifteenth century, more books directed at a youthful audience became available. William Caxton's printings of Reynard the Fox (1481) and Aesop's Fables (1484) were two of the more interesting in the series of otherwise didactic works which issued from his press.[1] For another several centuries, most works for children published in Europe or America provided instructions for good behavior or suggestions on how best to prepare for the world hereafter. Chapbooks, hornbooks, and primers, equally moralistic in tone, were designed to assist in the child's education. Not until the eighteenth century, when Mother Goose and the Arabian Nights stories first appeared in English translation and authors John Newbery and Oliver Goldsmith produced stories especially for children, did a significant body of works designed for children's reading pleasure emerge.

During the nineteenth century, the fairy tales of Wilhelm and Jacob Grimm and Hans Christian Andersen and books by Washington Irving, Charles Dickens, Sir Walter Scott, Louisa May Alcott, and others showed writing for children to be a growing area of activity. By the twentieth century, the number of authors who wrote exclusively for children notably increased. Moreover, the selection of topics covered in books for children ranged from humor, science, and natural history to poetry, hobbies, and adjustment to real-life situations.

Today, the amount of writings for children continues to rise, and the variety in topics treated demonstrates the continued concern for catering to all types of reading needs. The proportion of writings for children in relation to the total number of books published in the United States is also expanding. Figures for 1920 show children's books made up 7.71 percent of the total;[2] those for 1983 indicate juvenile works accounted for 11.49 percent.[3]

At the same time the number of books for children increased, the number of libraries and organizations for children and their special reading interests grew. The School Library Section of the National Education Association (NEA), founded in 1896, became one of the earliest organizations to recognize the importance of children and books. Later, in 1914, the American Library Association (ALA) assumed responsibility for representing school librarians at the national level through its American Association of School Librarians.

In 1900, soon after NEA's action, ALA established the Children's Services Division, called the Association for Library Services to Children since 1977. The year 1900 also marked the establishment of the first library to departmentalize children's services: the Carnegie Library of Pittsburgh.[4] People like Caroline Hewins, director of the Hartford Public Library and also responsible for opening a children's room at her library, and Anne Carroll Moore, supervisor of the children's department of the New York Public Library, did much to encourage children to love books and libraries and to develop special facilities for them.

During the 1920s and 30s, publishing houses which had previously brought out children's books "now and then on the side"[5] started special children's departments. Macmillan, first to provide the added service in 1919, was soon followed by Frederick Stokes (1922), Doubleday (1923), and later Viking (1933).[6] Noted children's editors like Louis Seaman, Helen Dean Fish, and May Massee encouraged authors and illustrators to produce books for children and to foster beauty, imagination, and inspiration in works written for the young reader.

Concurrent with the development of a children's literature and libraries or departments to meet their needs was an interest in specialized cataloging for such material. Announcement of the first special cataloging for children came at the 1902 ALA meeting when the Cleveland Public Library and Carnegie Library were assigned the task of preparing a list of juvenile subject headings, with the work appearing the next year.[7] Margaret Mann's *Subject Headings for Use in Dictionary Catalogs of Juvenile Books,* an effort to make the Pittsburgh headings consistent with the 1911 *ALA List of Subject Headings for Use in Dictionary Catalogs,* came out in 1916.

Changes in cataloging for children's books aimed partly to promote the "furthest possible use of a comparatively limited collection" and partly to eliminate unnecessary bibliographic details which made use of the catalog difficult.[8] Simplification of catalog use instruction, the need for specific subjects corresponding to school references, and even keeping children out of the way of adult readers proved additional reasons for modifying cataloging rules.

Another effort to make subject headings for children's materials more useful came in 1944 when Eloise Rue, in conducting research for a thesis, asked public school supervisors, children's librarians, curriculum specialists, and children's catalogers about the subject heading preferences of elementary school children.[9] (But she failed to ask the children.) The survey results appeared in 1952 when Rue and Effie LaPlante published *Subject Headings for Children's Literature.* In their preface, the authors introduced another important consideration—the child's vocabulary.

Children's interests are universal, but their vocabulary is still growing along with their learning processes, so subject headings which
anticipate their approach to a wide variety of material and which
employ terminology with which they are familiar are needed to
facilitate their use of the library catalog.[10]

Rue also recognized the need to keep close to standard cataloging
practice so that children would be ready to understand the adult
cata'og when the time came.

Despite the number of authors and organizations concerned with
the problem of children's cataloging and offering solutions, the difficulty of addressing children's special needs and reconciling practices
with increased standardization in cataloging procedures posed further
difficulties during the 1960s. In 1963, the Library of Congress established a Children's Book Section in its Reference Department to
provide bibliographical, reference, and research services to those who
serve children.[11] Earlier, in 1957, a special catalog of juvenile books
had been established at LC. The many deficiencies noted in this
catalog, especially after its removal to the new section, eventually
resulted in the 1966 establishment of the Children's Literature Cataloging Office with a senior cataloger from the Subject Cataloging
Division as its head. For the first time, the Library of Congress
furnished brief descriptive annotations (AC-Annotated Cards) on all
cards for children's materials, allowed fewer subdivisions denoting
juvenile material, supplied more subject headings for fiction and for
all types of books, and initiated the use of headings showing kind or
form.[12]

At the same time these changes took place at the Library of
Congress, members of ALA's Resources and Technical Services Division (RTSD) also showed concern for cataloging children's materials
by setting up an ad hoc discussion group at the 1967 New Orleans
Midwinter Meeting.[13] Librarians who attended the group's first ses-
sion at the ALA Annual Conference in San Francisco on June 25,
1967, expressed special interest in standardization ("compatibility,
not absolute uniformity") of the cataloging of library materials for
children.[14]

By 1968, the Cataloging and Classification Section of RTSD
announced a new Cataloging of Children's Materials Committee,
which agreed to urge uniform cataloging of children's materials
through the use of Library of Congress Cataloging as it appears on
MARC records and also to counsel the Library of Congress on
children's cataloging.[15] The committee continues to act as sounding
board and reactor.

ALA originally adopted The Library Bill of Rights in 1948.
Article V has included the word "age" since 1967: "A person's right
to use a library should not be denied or abridged because of origin,
age, background, or views." The added word reflected concern that

children might be denied access to library materials simply because librarians felt they weren't "ready" for them. However, some librarians also fear destructive behavior, resulting in damage to materials. So practices like permitting only teachers to check out read-along books with cassettes still exist. Conversely, a children's librarian recently refused to permit an adult to use the terminal in the children's room. Nor was the adult permitted to take software to the terminal in the library's adult section.

Despite the attention given the subject during the past 85 years, catalogers still have not met all of children's special needs, and they still mull over questions that concerned librarians in 1900. Every aspect is under scrutiny. Inglewood (CA) Public Library has adapted Library of Congress Classification in modified form for use with children's materials.[16] Yonkers (NY) Public Library and Carolyn W. Lima in *A to Zoo* have devised subject headings which bring out special concepts in children's picture books. Writers, among them Sanford Berman, Lois Chan, and Theodore Hines, have criticized current practices and sought solutions. Public and school library technical services divisions have in some cases created their own subject heading lists and modifications of standard lists to benefit their young clientele. (Exhibit 1 reproduces the thesaurus used by the Wichita [KS] public schools.) Much of the difficulty experienced in the past may be alleviated by developing a theoretical base for the cataloging of children's materials.

THEORY AND KNOWLEDGE BASE BEHIND PRACTICE

Perreault identified sound criteria for a well-developed theory of cataloging that also applies to children's cataloging. He maintained that the theory "would need to include a stout component of the purpose of and need for access consonant with the information needs of the population served."[17] An additional requirement is that retrieval respond maximally to access strategy. The question arises: Who possesses and can clearly articulate a well-developed theory of children's cataloging, one that integrates the functions of entry, description, subject heading application, classification, Cutter or book numbers, filing, and any other pertinent aspect? Furthermore, in order to develop a coherent theory and knowledge base, research methods for studying catalog use require reevaluation. Inappropriate research designs that destroy validity must not be perpetuated.

From what do practitioners presently derive a sense of "rightness" about how they catalog children's material? What corroborates for them what they may have read about, heard about, or learned about in library school from cataloging professors who may not have actually cataloged any children's materials or who may have given little or no attention to the Library of Congress Annotated Card (AC) Program principles and headings?

In an article describing a catalog of large-size cards that included book jacket illustrations and were designed for children in the beginning reading stage, one librarian outlined her decision-making process for assigning headings to certain picture books.

> I showed a group of cards to a child one day. They seemed to me to have something in common, and I said to her, "What are these all about?". . .She studied them for a while and said, "They're all about pretending." In our catalog, therefore, is the heading PRETEND-ING.[18]

A matter of crucial importance to the knowledge base for cataloging children's materials is the determination of "aboutness." Realistically, subjectivity will never be fully controlled when choosing headings. At least four studies have indicated that some differences in the application of subject headings to the books involved resulted not from the fault of a list but because those assigning the subject headings failed to recognize an item's subject or major emphasis.[19]

If librarians ask children for cataloging suggestions, they might also ask parents. What kinds of suggestions might come from parents? One small group provided these.

1. Make it possible to find books with Bugs Bunny in the catalog and to locate wordless picture books.
2. Make clear how the library defines "picture books."
3. Provide children with the rationale behind the library's moving books around (this from the mother of a little boy who had suffered near trauma from a library's frequent shelving rearrangements).
4. Consider ergonomics when organizing material by such means as having stuffed cushions or bean bags handy for children to sit on while browsing through items gathered from shelves (one library provides bunk beds in a loft for horizontal reading, another a bathtub to crawl in with a pillow for reading at most any angle).
5. Provide a catalog with large cards for children just learning to read, using book jackets and graphics to represent items and their contents.
6. Identify inherent difficulty of items by symbols 1, 2, and 3, rather than by age or grade level, as found in music for use by beginner, intermediate, or advanced students, regardless of age or educational level of the individual—or, in some other way, legitimize learning at appropriate levels at any point in a child's life.

Librarians at times regard beliefs and policies relative to children's cataloging as facts when they are based solely on informal observation and opinion. This decision-making procedure lends itself to patchwork "fixes" rather than to sound solutions. Whether or not their viewpoints later prove to be correct, intellectual integrity demands the investigation and consideration of further evidence, or at least an explicit recognition that further study might produce different results.

For example, a 1975 report of a meeting of the Cataloging of Children's Materials Committee betrayed the subtle shift from the child's to the cataloger's point of view:

> "In the following discussion the committee agreed that children are not really bothered by the changes on the cards and that better indexing, more examples, and a more extensive glossary in the new code would eliminate the need for an abridgment or simplification of it.[20]

Because hypotheses emerge from well-defined questions, honest awareness of what we know and do not know is an important first step toward building a knowledge and theory base for children's cataloging.

Objectives of Children's Cataloging and Catalogs

About 20 years ago, Rue commented that "the catalog cannot be everything to everyone."[21] What can it be, and what can the cataloging process mean to children and to the librarians, parents, educators, counselors, and others who share media and media catalogs with them? Back in the nineteenth century, Charles Cutter identified three main objectives for a library catalog, which he presumably intended for application to children's catalogs as well: "The old catalogs were not made for children, but the modern ones have to be, especially in a circulating library, for the children are the libraries' best clients."[22] The three objectives Cutter identified are (1) to enable a person to find a book of which any of the following is known: author, title, or subject; (2) to show what the library has by a given author, on a given subject, or in a given kind of literature; and (3) to assist in the choice of a book: as to its edition (bibliographically), or as to its character (literary or topical).[23]

On the other hand, Berman recommends "rigorous title-page cataloging"[24] in which Cutter's "known-item" function would be fulfilled, but not the "collocation" function, except through use of "see also" references. For example, Gail Hamilton, Barbara Corcoran, or Paige Dixon, all the same person, would be given a main entry according to the name on the title page. Although Perreault believes them to be performance criteria rather than principles of construction,[25] Berman offers three fundamental principles or objectives that ought to underlie both descriptive and subject cataloging, including children's cataloging.

1. Intelligibility. Bibliographic data, i.e., the substance and format of catalog entries, should be helpful to catalog users. And should make sense.

2. Findability. That is, access. It should be quick and fullsome. This involves the use of contemporary, familiar language; entering works under the author's title-page name; and assigning enough added entries—for title, subtitles, collaborators, and subjects—to make the material locatable where people are likely to look for it.

3. Fairness. That is, fairness to the material being cataloged and—in terms of subject cataloging in particular—to the topics themselves. For instance, it's *not* fair to the whole category of materials we call *audiovisual* or *nonprint* to either not catalog them at all or to treat them in a second-class way vis-à-vis books. And, as another instance, it's not fair to employ rubrics for ethnic groups that are not their *own,* preferred names.[26]

Berman translated these principles into a cataloging code dealing with vocabulary and assignment of subject headings for public, school, and community college libraries.[27] Prompted by perceived inadequacies in LC cataloging, Koger compiled principles from various sources, including the Berman code, to guide practice in assigning headings to children's fiction.[28]

Chan's treatment of objectives for a children's catalog refers to the primary catalog functions given in the 1965 edition of Piercy's *Commonsense Cataloging:* (1) as holdings record, so that the reader seeking a specific work quickly discovers whether or not it is in the library's collections, and (2) as location record to show the reader where the desired book is located. To these functions a third may be added, namely (3) reference uses to show (a) what the library has on a specific subject, and (b) what titles by a given author the library has.[29]

With respect to the objectives of catalogs of children's materials and their relation to ISBD principles and rules, Chan stated that children's catalogs' "different objectives and functions require different principles and rules."[30] The question arises: How are these objectives, which incorporate both the "known-item" and "collocation" functions, different from those set forth by Cutter for both juvenile and adult material?

Concerning ISBD principles and rules, and with reference to a paper written by Gorman, Chan stated, "We need not accept Gorman's principles, but we could apply his method of analyzing and of synthesizing as much of a consensus as possible from current practice to the development of a set of rules for school and small libraries."[31] Thus, rules would be derived from a codification of practice, but according to what principles?

Problems with objectives for the subject analysis of children's materials center around what constitutes a "subject heading" and what does not. Consider whether the following items belong in subject tracings, in the descriptive cataloging areas of the bibliographic record, in a field or subfield not yet established, or outside the bibliographic record in bibliographies, booklists, indexes, or printed subject heading lists that serve as guides to picture books: age, grade, and reader interest levels; literary genre; physical form; developmental values; curricular areas; themes; uses for material; multicultural designations, broadly defined to include disabled people, positive sex roles, and ethnic groups; literary and media awards; analytics; and characteristics of books as identified by Pollett—such as fluency, flexibility, originality, elaboration, and evaluation—that challenge productive thinking.[32]

About 20 years ago, Hines raised questions valid today concerning objectives of the classification function in relation to those of the subject heading function: "Do we want headings or classification by genre? Which and how? . . .Are we substituting subject heading work for classification, and, if so, does this indicate a need to revise classification? Do we want classification on the shelf or in the catalog?"[33] For instance, should picture books receive a genre "subject" heading when they are classified as picture books and shelved separately?

Discussion of the objectives of children's cataloging and catalogs could benefit from greater precision in the use of the word "objectives." "Objectives" need to be differentiated clearly from "principles," "performance criteria," "guidelines," "codes," etc. Both children's and adult cataloging would gain from this clarification. An understanding of the relation between the two is hampered by the unanswered questions and disagreements concerning exactly what the objectives of children's cataloging and catalogs are.

Relation of Children's Cataloging to Adult Cataloging

General items on cataloging in the professional literature rarely include references to children's cataloging except for an occasional brief description of the AC Program. Authors do not make explicit whether their writings are intended to apply as well to children's cataloging. In a 1974 article on the implications of ISBD for children's materials, Chan stated that "among the many questions raised, few concern the implications of the new format for the cataloging of children's literature."[34]

Critiques of cataloging found in the literature could be applied where appropriate to children's cataloging. For example, Pejtersen and Austin's 1983 study reporting the development and evaluation of a system for organizing fiction based on an analysis of users' formulations of needs stirs thinking relative to the organization of children's fiction.[35] Less recently, Kirtland and Cochrane compiled a bibliographic essay covering the period of post-World War II to 1979 in which they listed LCSH weaknesses or defects, suggested improvements, and the critic and/or suggestor with date. The suggested improvements that LC has not yet addressed warrant study for possible application to the subject analysis of children's material.[36] Wilson's 1979 article on specificity is a critique of systematic duplication of entries at specific and generic levels.[37] The AC Program follows this practice, which merits review in light of Wilson's comments.

The overall cataloging function in all types of libraries basically serves the same purposes according to Intner: "The facts don't support the belief that acquisition, cataloging and classification, and circulation in public or school libraries are inherently different from the same functions in academic, research, or special libraries."[38]

Are children's materials sufficiently different from adult materials to warrant special treatment? The appearance of this essay in a book on cataloging special materials supports the view that children's materials are special materials. *Library Literature* treats children's cataloging as a special subject, under "Subject headings--Special subjects--Children's literature," listed alphabetically among other subdivisions like "Business" and "Geology." In a 1965 critique of the revised classification system developed by librarians in the Boys and Girls Division of the Toronto Public Libraries, Jones raised this fundamental question.

> The basic difficulty experienced with this system and others similar to it which have appeared in library literature is with the *rationale* for development—that a special classification system is needed for children's books because they are somehow different from books written for adults. How are they different?[39]

The "Guidelines for Standardized Cataloging of Children's Materials" present a different view. These were developed by the Cataloging of Children's Materials Committee of the RTSD Cataloging and Classification Section and accepted by the RTSD Board of Directors in 1982. The "Guidelines" codified the 1969 recommendation by the Cataloging of Children's Materials Committee, subsequently adopted by ALA/RTSD's Cataloging and Classification Section, that the Library of Congress Annotated Card (AC) Program for children's materials established in 1966 be adopted as a national standard. Juvenile works were regarded as those for use by children through junior-high level. The "Guidelines" state: "The library community has long recognized that the users of children's materials have their unique characteristics and requirements. This class of materials, which includes print and nonprint formats, was considered different enough to warrant special bibliographic treatment to meet the needs of the audiences for which it was intended."[40] Nonetheless, the AC Program aimed to meet the needs of child users in a way which is compatible with adult cataloging: "As a further benefit, by making children's cataloging compatible with that for adult materials without sacrificing its unique characteristics, these standards will help lead the young user to understand the adult card catalog and its successors."[41]

The AC Program was developed according to the following procedure: "In the absence of any theoretical research, user studies, or general agreements on the 'best' subject headings for children, the catalogers had to substitute intuition, frequent consultation of the Sears list and authorities in the field, and common sense for a master plan of subject heading development."[42] Ironically, the 1983 third edition of *Commonsense Cataloging* made no reference to the AC Program, mentioning only that "small public and school libraries usually take their headings from Sears."[43]

The principles of application that emerged from the Library of Congress Children's Literature Cataloging Office through the process of subject heading development are as follows: (1) elimination of subdivisions such as JUVENILE FICTION, (2) use of subject headings for most fiction, (3) more generous use of subject headings, often including the use of both a specific and a general heading, and (4) use of headings denoting form or kind: JOKE BOOKS, MYSTERY STORIES, etc.[44]

The issue of whether children's cataloging should use different cataloging tools from those used for adult materials is a longstanding one. The "Guidelines" recommend following the second level of description as found in Rule 1.0D2 in *AACR2,* including dimensions, other statements of responsibility (such as illustrator), and series. In addition, the General Material Designation (GMD) is required for certain types of materials, including chart, kit, realia, diorama, microform, slide, filmstrip, microscope slide, sound recording, flash card, model, transparency, game, motion picture, and video recording. The only note required is the summary, and the International Standard Book Number (ISSN) is mandated when available. Berman asks, on the other hand, "If annotations have proven useful on juvenile entries, why not do the same for adult titles?"[45]

Truett views the use of the *AACR2* rules as particularly amenable to school library situations. She believes that they facilitate the creation of integrated collections of various media formats and prepare for the time when automated cataloging becomes more universally available.[46] Thus she recommends use of the full *AACR2* rather than the abridged edition.[47] The actual use of *AACR2* in school libraries is another matter. Truett surveyed 200 randomly chosen media specialists in Nebraska, with these results:

"Librarians were as likely to use AACR1 as they were AACR2 for main entry choice and they were even more likely to use some authority other than either of these. Indeed, responses to this question indicated that some librarians may not have actually understood what is meant by main entry as they cited Dewey and Sears as their authorities. Many apparently were of the opinion that no rules are necessary for main entry choice, as almost one-fifth use none."[48]

Few may think of the Library of Congress Classification scheme as applicable to children's collections, but the "Guidelines" permit use of this system or the Dewey Decimal Classification through the first prime mark which indicates the abridged number. This is the standard as well for nonfiction picture and primary books, rather than a letter or number scheme that may somewhat duplicate the subject heading function, such as those presented by Williams and Barker, respectively.[49] The Inglewood (CA) Public Library, as mentioned earlier, adapted LC classification for children's library materials. It uses two letters followed by one or two numbers when more detail is required. According to the library director, "librarians, teachers, and children find the system easy to use."[50]

Unlike the decision regarding the abridged Dewey, the *Sears List of Subject Headings* was not adopted as the standard subject heading list although it was considered to be "in large measure an abridgment of the LC list."[51] In fact, publication of another list had originally seemed unnecessary because the AC Program differed from adult cataloging practices largely in application, rather than in terminology.[52] However, in response to pressure from the library community, the Library of Congress published *Subject Headings for Children's Literature: A Statement of Principles of Application and a List of Headings That Vary from Those Used for Adult Literature* in 1969. The list is updated and cumulated in regular LCSH supplements.[53] Beginning with the Winter 1982 issue, the *Cataloging Service Bulletin* contains "as a regular feature a list of new subject headings that represent popular trends or concepts."[54]

Speaking against formulation of the AC subject headings list, Berman asked,

Why catalog kids' stuff separately?. . .Some children's works, of course, demand special handling since they deal with topics that don't appear in adult-oriented literature. But that only requires the formulation of accurate, appropriate headings to mirror those topics, the new forms then entering the *total* thesaurus.[55]

Berman echoed the words of Prevost back in 1952: "If our standard list of subject headings is based upon wise and clear principles, that list should be used for all of our catalogs; and the principles governing it should be taught to all users, be they children, teenagers, or adults."[56] The AC Program, however, chose to differ in principles of application as well as through its AC subject headings. The relation of children's cataloging to adult cataloging could benefit from further clarification. Both descriptive cataloging and subject analysis require attention.

Standardization of Children's Cataloging

A dilemma in children's cataloging that must be examined concerns standardization. Early leaders in the AC Program regarded standardization as an especially important benefit, and they were opposed to acceptance of nonstandard cataloging practices from a variety of sources. They also took into consideration the development of bibliographic utilities and the MARC program to provide dissemination. However, as Rose interpreted the "Guidelines," "this does not mean that libraries or cataloging agencies must use LC cataloging or purchase LC cards, but that to conform to the standard, original cataloging from whatever source must follow the same principles used in AC cataloging."[57]

The "Guidelines" intend "sufficient latitude for the individual cataloger or library to meet local needs while remaining within the standards. The elements recommended in these guidelines are intended to meet the needs of the users, in accordance with the purpose of the catalog record."[58] But it is not clear whether the purpose of the catalog record was considered identical for both children's and adult material.

Does this interpretation mean, therefore, that standardization has not been violated if a librarian adds SLEEP to the AC headings for Dr. Seuss's *Sleep Book*, changes TOY AND MOVABLE BOOKS to POP-UP BOOKS, changes TAIL--FICTION to TAILS--FICTION for *The Magnificent Morris Mouse Clubhouse* [Gibbons], adds BIGFOOT MONSTERS to a book about various Bigfoot monsters, changes OBSTINACY to STUBBORNNESS, adds NEW BABY for Alexander's *When the Baby Comes, I'm Moving Out*, or adds ACCIDENTS--FICTION for Baker's *Benjamin's Book*?

Are the familiar contributions from Hennepin County Library relative to juvenile cataloging within the AC Program standards because they follow the established principles? Do librarians add to or modify subject heading tracings assigned in the AC Program because they're responding to identified local needs? Or do they change subject tracings because they regard them as unacceptable and provide instead a set they approve (which, incidentally, could well have been provided by the AC Program catalogers)?

In a 1980 article, Hines, Winkel, and Collins reviewed their pilot study of a data bank for children's media. Possible future activities included development of a turnkey microcomputer system for distribution of programs and copies of the data bank material on disks for local search.[59] In a later article, Hines and Winkel proposed the development of a computer-produced cataloging and information access scheme for children's media which "combines the most useful aspects of library subject-heading lists and thesauri with some unique aspects, and meets. . .the American Library Association recommendations for the subject cataloging of juvenile materials."[60]

An implied objective of the Children's Media Data Bank project is the production of acceptable, immediately useful cataloging products. As Berman points out, "Unless there is some special bibliographic center for creating and distributing cataloging for public and other nonresearch libraries, three levels of description or any other optional routes place the burden squarely on the individual libraries."[61] Do librarians want standardization in principle or in fact? If the latter, desired performance criteria would be compiled and applied consistently.

Relation of Children's Cataloging to Other Library Functions

The legitimacy for children's services librarians to devote some time to cataloging-related matters rests on the assumption that there is a symbiotic type of relationship between placing and finding materials. The 1969 recommendations made by the Committee on the Cataloging of Children's Materials appear to be based on the philosophy that the children's services librarian is to be entirely excluded from all aspects of the cataloging function, including necessary feedback to catalogers:

> These recommendations emerge from the firm belief that children's needs are served only when their librarians devote full energy and attention to the selection and use of materials. Librarians who work with, and in the interest of, children have neither the time nor the expertise to catalog the quantity and variety of materials called for in professional standards and in the Report of the National Advisory Commission on Libraries. When children's or school librarians are diverted from their primary responsibility to engage in cataloging operations, then effort is duplicated, and service to children is diluted.[62]

Hines corroborated this view:

> For all too many children's services people, Cataloging-in-Publication and centralized cataloging seem to have offered the opportunity to spend more time than original cataloging would require to second guess and change the decisions made by the experts—mainly for the worse. This preoccupation with where a book is placed in the collection rather than the ability to retrieve it wherever placed, is one of the largest time wasters in librarianship."[63]

Thus, some catalogers may picture themselves as belonging to a knowledgeable elite group of experts. In turn, some children's services librarians may not want anything to do with cataloging. These attitudes, where they exist, stand in the way of improving children's cataloging.

TRANSITION STAGE

Persisting throughout the above analysis of theoretical areas, including objectives, the relation of children's to adult cataloging, standardization, and the relation of juvenile cataloging to other library functions, is the issue of whether there are bona fide user needs on the local level which can be met only by departing from national level cataloging. With reference to Cutter's insistence that the convenience of the public should not yield to the convenience of the bibliographical system, Dunkin pointed out that "the user, however, is hard, if not impossible, to identify. He [sic] stands there only in shadowy outline as we try to psychoanalyze him [sic]. Consequently, we cannot construct a truly logical and orderly bibliographical system. All we can do is accumulate a set of practices."[64]

To understand the child user, is it enough to ask, "What is a child?" and let cataloging reflect that generic child? Instead, is the individual child more important? Or is the more pertinent question, "Is there one or more specialized groups of children who use this particular library?" Should all three questions be considered? No wonder librarians find it difficult to see the child user in other than shadowy outline. Fine brings the problem into focus: "As it stands now, behavioral research in librarianship. . .does not deal with the essence of library service, the way human beings process and use information. In its current state, behavioral research in librarianship is not leading toward the development of a theory of user behavior.[65]

More specifically, Fine claims that

> people come to libraries to solve problems. . .not to 'find information'. . . .Libraries are really in the business of fulfilling a psychological need, presupposing that human beings have a 'need' for information for social survival, to be productive, and for their personal growth. . . .Librarians need to understand the process by which people come to experience their need for information—how they acquire it, unconsciously process it, consciously manipulate it, and then make use of it—before they can create a psychologically-relevant information environment.[66]

It's within this behavioral context that children's librarians and those who catalog children's materials must together conduct their research on how to determine and satisfy the child user's cataloging needs at local and national levels. They can study responses to the online public access catalog to produce substantial insight and knowledge about child user behavior. Computer searches cannot be analyzed, however, unless librarians insist that programs be written so that needed information may be captured, especially the search strategies used to obtain particular outcomes, and that capability for search strategies to be tested are built in. Gordon's plaint may be answered more satisfactorily and with more far-reaching implications than could be provided by exercise of common sense alone: "The awkward circumstance of the card catalog or book, fiche, and automated catalogs, is their inability to meet common thought processes."[67]

Against the present backdrop of theoretical ambiguity, librarians would be hard pressed to reflect local specialized needs of younger patrons in online public access catalogs, as Sager discussed in an article on library service to the microchip generation. He noted as a problem

> the standardization of subject headings, which may limit the library's capability to design specialized headings relevant to its younger patrons. This would occur, not due to the limitations of the computer, which could grant almost infinite flexibility, but due to economics. The local library, which could catalog its resources to reflect local variations, may find it more convenient to accept standardized computer produced cataloging rather than go through the expense of customizing access to its holdings. . . .Even with online catalogs, the policies of the cooperative or larger system may prevent the local library from making these changes to suit the specialized needs ot its younger patrons."[68]

The dilemma Sager expressed will be felt increasingly. A number of software programs are on the market for producing online catalogs, some with enhancements to make use possible for even younger children. Larger school districts may tie use of microcomputer catalogs into a bibliographic utility.

> School libraries, and particularly those in large districts, are moving toward automation in their cataloging services and are consequently joining a network such as OCLC which uses both LC and AACR2 rules. Mountain View Elementary School in Northglen, Colorado, is an example of an individual school with a microcomputer library catalog tied into the OCLC database, and Westside Community School District in Omaha, Nebraska, is representative of an entire district that is converting over to an automated system via OCLC.[69]

The cooperative projects Sager mentioned are exemplified in Wisconsin, where over 60 individual schools or school districts are using MITINET, a microcomputer automation system that makes available a county-wide union catalog enabling all the public and school libraries to determine whether a title is held in the county, where it is held, and what the local call number is.[70] Call numbers may vary in book numbers if not in the class notation.

Lead time will be required for the accomplishment of productive studies to clarify issues. As Hines and Winkel pointed out, "Although knowledgeable librarians occasionally use heading lists as aids in searching, the lists are not basically designed for this purpose and their use in searching is neither usual nor usually known to library users."[71] This situation will predictably change with the advent of microcomputer catalogs. Children's reader services librarians will likely use the classification and subject heading tools to an unprecedented extent for subject access. These librarians will provide feedback on browsing display formats to sources of tape versions of the cataloging tools. Searches on bibliographic records could include the use of Boolean strategies with uncontrolled as well as controlled headings on desired fields of the bibliographic record. Terms in headings lists and in search strategies could be designated as primary or secondary in importance.

Records may be linked to authority file entries with coordinated, even global, updates. Complete listings of downward "see also" references could be particularly useful in Boolean strategies involving the "not" operator to relieve the searcher of identifying numerous individual items. Special listings, such as reading ladders in a desired area, could be produced. Interfaces with other computerized information tools and services, as well as with other library functions, such as circulation, may exist.

Various search strategies and outcomes may be compared and evaluated. Dewey numbers that extend past the prime mark may receive new interest as a means of avoiding excessive output. The review of recorded searching procedures captured on tape through programs modified for this purpose could yield suggestions to the AC Program for "see" references or new subject headings. Reports about catalog use and motivation can go beyond the generalized statements that have characterized descriptions of child use or avoidance of the traditional card catalog.

Will children fully exploit microcomputer catalogs? At least two reasons indicate that they will not only benefit from this catalog format but will also enjoy the experience. First, children have become accustomed to using microcomputers at home or at school, very likely in the library, for curricular units. Because of the interactive characteristic of computer software, Fasick believes that "children who learn to work with computers tend to develop an attitude toward learning which is different from that of children who are educated solely through books. The computer invites participation and exploration.[72] Thus, children will take more initiative in pursuing learning.

Second, instruction in searching microcomputer catalogs has yet to draw on the largely untapped resources available through research in educational psychology and its applications, especially in the language arts. For example, research on teaching and learning the concept of classes and collections in hierarchical relations, which center around Piaget's theories, can be applied to any context in which children use taxonomic categories, including library subject heading and classification structures. How children interpret, represent, and use hierarchical organization is an important area in child development.[73] Three instructional strategies for vocabulary development—semantic associations, semantic mapping, and semantic feature analysis—stress relationships and involve classification.[74] These strategies lend themselves well to instruction on the syndetic structure of catalogs, as well as the hierarchical arrangement of Dewey.

The analysis of procedure and outcomes of children's online catalog use is an essential component of needed behavioral research on how children seek, process, and use library materials and information. Hypotheses and ultimately a theory and knowledge base for children's cataloging may emerge. The objectives of children's cataloging and catalogs, the relation of children's cataloging to adult cataloging, the standardization of children's cataloging, including the concept of "local needs," and the relation of children's cataloging to other library functions may become clear. Purposes of descriptive cataloging and subject analysis may be more rigorously defined. Cataloging and retrieval options for adult and child accessing of children's catalogs, as well as for browsing and location needs, may develop.

It will not be necessary, however, to wait for a distant date in order to make improvements in children's cataloging. Results of pilot projects and small, manageable studies will cumulate, not as patchwork "fixes," but within broad conceptual goals. Immediate practical benefits can be put to use and tested further. Librarians need to keep abreast of changes in the computer field. At least one school library's microcomputer catalog is limited in the number of spaces that can be taken up by a subject heading, with adverse effects on searching. This practice reflects limitations of earlier computer generations and programming techniques, not present capabilities. On the other hand, the librarian in charge of cataloging for a large school district about to install public access catalogs has another outlook. He finds "ideas gestating, ideas we didn't know could exist."

Children's cataloging will not improve, especially with respect to subject analysis, unless librarians are motivated to improvement. In addition, budget restrictions may be a problem. It is important that cost be viewed in relation to user benefits. One vendor reported the following experience.

> Recently, Brodart experimented with *in-depth subject headings.* We took a basic list of school titles from one of the Wilson publications, examined these works, and enhanced it with additional subject headings—as many as 50—but with an average of 13 subject headings per title. In addition, we used current language to assign subjects. . . .But, it does cost money to do this and we did *not* have a response from the public to pay for it."[75]

However, librarians may expect motivation from an unexpected source. Foskett has warned, "I also believe that the time when our readers will no longer tolerate the kind of folly we now impose on them is approaching."[76] With their serious interest and increasing participation in computerized retrieval of library material, and their growing initiative in directing their own learning, children themselves may well be responsible for a number of constructive suggestions for improved cataloging.

EXHIBIT 1
Wichita Public Schools: Subject Headings for Special Education and Library Media Therapy (December 1984)

ACCEPTANCE
ACTING
ACTIVITIES
ADAPTABILITY
ADOLESCENCE
ADOPTION
ADVENTURE AND
   ADVENTURERS
AERONAUTICS
AFRO-AMERICANS
AGING
AIRPLANES
AMISH
ANGER
APARTMENT HOUSES
APPRECIATION OF OTHERS
ART
ART AND NATURE
ARTS AND CRAFTS
ASSERTIVENESS
ATHLETICS
ATTENTION
ATTITUDES
AUTOMOBILES

BABY SITTERS
BACKPACKING
BALLADS
BALLET
BASEBALL
BASKETBALL
BEAUTY
BEDTIME

BEHAVIOR
BELONGING
BIBLE STORIES
BICYCLES
BILINGUAL
BIRTHDAYS
BLIND
BLIND--AIDS
BOASTFULNESS
BODY AWARENESS
BOOK TALKS
BOXING
BOY-GIRL RELATIONS
BOY SCOUTS
BRAVERY
BULLIES
BURIED TREASURE

CAMP FIRE GIRLS
CAMPING
CAREERS
CAREFULNESS
CARTOONS
CATHOLIC CHURCH
CEREBRAL PALSY
CHANGE
CHARACTER BUILDING
CHEERFULNESS
CHILD ABUSE
CHRISTIANITY
CHRISTMAS
CIRCUS
CITIZENSHIP

CITY LIFE
CIVIL RIGHTS
CLEANLINESS
CLEVERNESS
CLUBS
COLLECTING
COLORS
COMMUNICATION
COMPANION TO. . .
COMPASSION
COMPETENCE
COMPUTERS
CONCEIT
CONCEPT AWARENESS
CONFLICT
CONTRARINESS
COOKING
COOPERATION
COPING
COUNTRY LIFE
COURAGE
COURTESY
COWHANDS
CREATIVE EXPRESSION
CRIME AND CRIMINALS
CULTS
CURIOSITY

DANCING
DEAF
DEATH
DEMOCRACY
DEPRESSIONS
DISABLED
DISABLED--AIDS
DISASTERS
DIVORCE
DOLLS
DREAMS

EARLY CHILDHOOD
EARTH SCIENCE
EASTER
ECONOMIC DIFFERENCES
ECONOMICS
EDUCABLE MENTALLY
    HANDICAPPED

EDUCABLE MENTALLY
    HANDICAPPED--AIDS
EMOTIONAL SECURITY
EMOTIONS
ENERGY
ENVIRONMENTAL
    CONCEPTS
ETIQUETTE
EXERCISE
EXPLOITATION OF
    CHILDREN

FABLES
FAIRY TALES
FAMILY LIFE
FANTASIES
FARM LIFE
FATHER-DAUGHTER
    RELATIONS
FATHER-SON RELATIONS
FEARS
FESTIVALS
FINGER PLAYS
FOLKLORE
FOOTBALL
FOSTER HOME CARE
4-H CLUBS
FREEDOM
FRIENDS, SOCIETY OF
FRIENDSHIP
FRONTIER AND PIONEER
    LIFE

GAMES
GANGS
GENEROSITY
GHOST STORIES
GIFTED, TALENTED,
    CREATIVE
GIFTED, TALENTED,
    CREATIVE--AIDS
GIRL SCOUTS
GLOBAL PERSPECTIVES
GOALS
GOD
GRANDPARENTS
GREEDINESS

GROOMING, PERSONAL
GROWING UP (Used with
    Human Beings)
GROWTH (Used with Plants
    and Other Animals than
    Human Beings)
GUILT, FEELINGS OF
GYMNASTICS

HABIT
HALLOWEEN
HANDICRAFT
HANUKKAH
HAPPINESS
HEALTH
HEARING IMPAIRED
HELPFULNESS
HIBERNATION
HIKING
HISPANICS
HOBBIES
HOCKEY
HOLIDAYS
HONESTY
HOSPITALS
HUMAN RELATIONS
HUMOR

ILLNESS
IMAGINATION
INSPIRATION
INTEGRATION
INTUITION

JEALOUSY
JESUS CHRIST
JEWS
JOGGING
JOKES
JUSTICE

KANSAS
KANSAS AUTHORS
KIDNAPPING
KINDNESS
KINDNESS TO ANIMALS
KITES

KNIGHTS

LARGE PRINT
LAW
LAZINESS
LEADERSHIP
LEARNING
LEARNING DISABILITIES
LEARNING
    DISABILITIES--AIDS
LEGENDS
LIBRARIES
LIBRARY MEDIA CENTERS
    (SCHOOLS)
LIMERICKS
LISTENING
LITERATURE (Used with
    professional books only)
LONELINESS
LOVE
LOYALTY

MAGIC
MAINSTREAMING
MANNERS AND CUSTOMS
MAPS
MARIONETTES
MARRIAGE
MARTIAL ARTS
MATERIAL SECURITY
MEDITATIONS
MENNONITES IN THE U.S.
MENTAL ILLNESS
MEXICANS IN THE U.S.
MIGRANT LABOR
MONEY
MONSTERS
MOTHER-DAUGHTER
    RELATIONS
MOTHER-SON RELATIONS
MOTIVATION
MOVEMENT EDUCATION
MOVIE-TV TIE-INS
MOVING
MULTICULTURAL (MC)
MUSIC
MUSIC AND LITERATURE

MUSICAL INSTRUMENTS
MYSTERY STORIES
MYSTICISM
MYTHOLOGY

NATIVE AMERICANS
NATURAL SCIENCE
NEIGHBORS
NIGHT
NONSENSE
NUMBER CONCEPTS
NUTRITION

OBSERVATION
OCEANOGRAPHY
OCCULT SCIENCES
OLDER-YOUNGER
    RELATIONS
OLYMPIC GAMES
ONLY CHILD
ORAL HISTORY
ORIENTALS
ORPHANS
ORTHOPEDICALLY
    IMPAIRED
OUTDOOR LIFE

PANTOMIMES
PAPER ENGINEERING
PARENTING
PARTIES
PASSOVER
PATIENCE
PATRIOTISM
PEACE
PEER RELATIONS
PERSEVERANCE
PETS
PHOTOGRAPHY
PHYSICAL SCIENCE
PICNICS
PICTURE WRITING
PIRATES
PLAY
PLAYS
POETIC PROSE
POETRY

POSITIONS IN SPACE
POSITIVE SEX ROLE (PSR)
POVERTY
PRAYERS
PREHISTORIC ANIMALS
PREJUDICE
PREQUEL TO. . .
PRIDE
PRISONS
PRIVACY, NEED FOR
PROBLEM SOLVING
PROTESTANTISM
PROVERBS
PUPPETS
PUZZLES

RAINBOWS
RAINY DAY FUN
READ ALOUD
RECREATION
RED CROSS
REJECTION
RELIGION
RESOURCEFULNESS
RESPONSIBILITY
REST
RHYTHM
RIDDLES
ROBOTS
ROLE PLAYING
ROMANCE
RUNAWAYS

SABBATH
SAFETY
SCHOOL LIFE
SCIENCE FICTION
SCIENTIFIC METHOD
SEASONS
SECRETS
SECURITY
SEQUEL TO. . .
SELF CONCEPT
SELF EVALUATION
SELFISHNESS
SELF RELIANCE
SENSES

SEPARATION, MARITAL
SEXUALITY
SHADOW PLAYS
SHAKERS
SHAPES AND SIZES
SHARING
SHYNESS
SIBLINGS
SIGN LANGUAGE
SINGING GAMES
SINGLE-PARENT FAMILY
SKATING
SKIING
SKITS
SLAVERY
SLEEP
SOCCER
SOCIAL ADJUSTMENT
SONGS
SOUTHEAST ASIANS (Brunei,
    Burma, Cambodia, Laos,
    Malaysia, Philippines,
    Singapore, Thailand, Viet
    Nam, Indonesia)
SPACE AND TIME
SPACE TRAVEL
SPECIAL OLYMPICS
SPEECH IMPAIRED
SPEECH IMPAIRED--AIDS
SPIES
SPIRITUAL SECURITY
SPORTS
SPORTSMANSHIP
STEPPARENTS
STORMS
STORYTELLING
STUNTS
SUBSTANCE ABUSE
SUCCESS
SUICIDE
SUPERNATURAL
SUPERSTITION
SURVIVAL
SUSPENSE
SWIMMING

TALL TALES
TEACHING
TEASING
TECHNOLOGY
TEMPTATION
TENNIS
TIME
TONGUE TWISTERS
TOOLS
TOYS
TRAGEDY
TRAINS
TRANSPORTATION
TRAVELING
TRICKS
TRUSTWORTHINESS
TRUTHFULNESS

UNEMPLOYMENT
UNITED NATIONS
UNSELFISHNESS
UNSOLVED MYSTERIES
URBAN-RURAL CONTRASTS

VACATIONS
VIOLENCE
VISUAL LITERACY
VISUALLY IMPAIRED

WALKING
WAR
WEAPONS
WEATHER
WELLNESS
WICHITA AUTHORS
WISHES
WITCHCRAFT
WONDER
WOOD CARVING
WORDLESS BOOKS
WORDS
WORK
WORRY
WRESTLING
WRITING

REFERENCES

1. Cornelia Meigs, "Up to 1840; Roots in the Past," in *A Critical History of Children's Literature*, rev. ed., by Cornelia Meigs, et al. (New York: Macmillan, 1969), p. 29.

2. *Bowker Annual of Library and Book Trade Information, 1962.* (New York: Bowker, 1961), p. 59.

3. *Bowker Annual of Library and Book Trade Information, 1985.* (New York, Bowker, 1985), p. 460.

4. Florence W. Butler, "Children's Libraries and Librarianship," in *Encyclopedia of Library and Information Science*, 1st ed. S. r.: 562.

5. Elizabeth Gray Vining, "Nothing Too Much, Not Even Moderations," *Library School Review* (Kansas Teachers College) (May 1973): 8.

6. Ruth Hill Viguers, "1920-1967 Golden Years and Time of Tumult," in *A Critical History of Children's Literature*, rev. ed. by Cornelia Meigs et al. (New York: Macmillan, 1969), p. 392.

7. Elva Sophronia Smith et al. *Subject Headings for Children's Books in Public Libraries and in Libraries in Elementary and Junior High Schools.* (Chicago: American Library Association, 1933), p. viii.

8. Ibid.

9. Eloise Rue and Effie LaPlante, *Subject Headings for Children's Materials.* (Chicago: American Library Association, 1952), p. v.

10. Ibid.

11. Edmond L. Applebaum, "Library of Congress Annotated Cards for Children's Literature," *Library Resources & Technical Services* 10 (Fall 1966): 455.

12. Applebaum, p. 456.

13. American Library Association, *Proceedings of the 1967 Midwinter Meeting, New Orleans, Louisiana, January 9-14, 1967, and the 86th Annual Conference, San Francisco, California, June 25-July 1, 1967.* (Chicago: American Library Association, 1967), p. 101.

14. American Library Association, 1967, p. 234.

15. American Library Association, *Proceedings of the 87th Annual Conference, 1968, Kansas City, Missouri, June 23-29, 1968.* (Chicago: American Library Association, 1968), p. 182.

16. Inglewood Public Library. *Library of Congress Classification Adapted for Children's Library Materials.* (Inglewood, CA: Inglewood Public Library, 1976).

17. J. M. Perreault, "A Representative of the New Left in American Subject Cataloguing." A review essay on Sanford Berman's *The Joy of Cataloging*, with response by Sanford Berman. Occasional Papers, no. 161. (Champaign, IL: University of Illinois, Graduate School of Library and Information Science, 1983), p. 8.

18. Isabel Wilner, "Primary Catalog—Idea for Young Media Center Users," *School Media Quarterly* 2 (Summer 1974): 370.

19. Florence DeHart, "'Standardization in Commercial Children's Cataloging: A Comparative Study of 100-odd Titles," *Library Journal* 95 (February 15, 1970): 744-49; Florence DeHart, "The Disabled and Multiple Sensibilities in Children's Books," *Technicalities* 3 (September 1983): 10-11, 14; Florence DeHart and Marylouise Meder, "Piaget, Picture Storybooks, and Subject Access," *Technicalities* 5 (March 1985): 3-5, 16; Florence DeHart and Ellen Searles, "Developmental Values as Catalog Access Points for Children's Fiction," *Technicalities* 5 (January 1985): 13-15.

20. Lois Doman Rose, "RTSD CCS Cataloging of Children's Materials Committee," *LC Information Bulletin* 34 (August 15, 1975): A-189.

21. Eloise Rue, "Economy in the Catalog," *Library Journal* 91 (October 15, 1966): 5130.

22. Charles A. Cutter, *Rules for a Dictionary Catalog,* 4th ed. (Washington, DC: Government Printing Office, 1904), p. 6.

23. Cutter, p. 12.

24. Sanford Berman, "Follies & Deficiencies: LC's Cataloging of Children's Materials," *School Library Journal* 22 (April 1976): 50.

25. Perreault, p. 6.

26. Sanford Berman, "Cataloging for Public Libraries," in *The Nature and Future of the Catalog,* edited by Maurice J. Freedman and S. Michael Malinconico (Phoenix, AZ: Oryx Press, 1979), p. 225–26.

27. Sanford Berman, "A Subject Cataloging Code for Public, School, and Community College Libraries—A Proposal," *The U*N*A*B*A*S*H*E*D Librarian* 32 (1979), 19–20.

28. Ellen Koger, "Subject Headings for Children's Fiction," *Technical Services Quarterly* 2 (Fall/Winter 1984): 14.

29. Lois Mai Chan, "ISBD: Implications for Cataloging Children's Materials," *Children's Media Quarterly* 3 (Fall 1974); p. 23.

30. Chan, p. 26.

31. Ibid.

32. Nancy Polette, *Picture Books for Gifted Programs* (Metuchen, NJ: Scarecrow Press, 1981), p. 66.

33. Theodore C. Hines, "Crisis in Children's Cataloging," *Library Journal* 91 (September 15, 1966): 4186.

34. Chan, p. 21.

35. Annelise Mark Pejtersen and Jutta Austin, "Fiction Retrieval: Experimental Design and Evaluation of a Search System Based on Users' Value Criteria (Part 1)," *Journal of Documentation* 39 (December 1983): 230–46.

36. Monika Kirtland and Pauline Cochrane, "Critical Views of LCSH—Library of Congress Subject Headings," *Cataloging & Classification Quarterly* 1 (February/March 1982): 71–94.

37. Patrick Wilson, "The End of Specificity," *Library Resources & Technical Services* 23 (Spring 1979): 116–22.

38. Sheila A. Intner, "A Giant Step Backward for Technical Services," *Library Journal* 110 (April 15, 1985): 44.

39. Milbrey L. Jones, "Classifying Children's Books," *Library Resources & Technical Services* 9 (Spring 1965): 247.

40. "Guidelines for Standardized Cataloging of Children's Materials," *Top of the News* 40 (Fall 1983): 49.

41. "Guidelines," p. 50.

42. Treva Turner, "Cataloging Children's Materials at the Library of Congress," *The Quarterly Journal of the Library of Congress* 30 (April 1973): 153–54.

43. Rosalind E. Miller and Jane C. Terwillegar, *Commonsense Cataloging: A Cataloger's Manual,* 3d ed. (New York: Wilson, 1983), p. 4.

44. Turner, p. 154.

45. Berman, 1976, p. 50.

46. Carol Truett, "AACR Who? The Case for Using the New Anglo-American Cataloguing Rules in the School Library Media Center," *School Library Media Quarterly* 12 (Fall 1983): 41–42.

47. Michael Gorman, *The Concise AACR2.* (Chicago: American Library Association, 1981).

48. Carol Truett, "Is Cataloging a Passe Skill in Today's Technological Society?," *Library Resources & Technical Services* 28 (July/September 1984): 273.

49. Dianne T. McAfee, "The Young Child Uses the Media Center," *Language Arts* 53 (February 1976): 123–24; and Diane Barker, "Color It Easy," *School Media Quarterly* 7 (Spring 1979): 221–23.

50. John W. Perkins, "An Adapted Library of Congress Classification for Children's Materials," *Library Resources & Technical Services* 22 (Spring 1978): 178.

51. Lois Doman Rose, "LC's National Standard for Cataloging Children's Materials: Explanation," *School Library Journal* 22 (January 1976): 22.

52. Applebaum, p. 458.

53. Turner, p. 154–55.

54. "Subject Headings of Current Interest," *Cataloging Services Bulletin* 19 (Winter 1982): 3-5.

55. Berman, 1976, p. 50.

56. Marie Louise Prevost, "Selection and Standards of Subject Headings for Use in Public Libraries," *Journal of Cataloging and Classification* 8 (December 1952): 135–36.

57. Rose, 1976, p. 20.

58. "Guidelines," p. 50.

59. Theodore C. Hines; Lois Winkel; and Rosann Collins, "The Children's Media Data Bank," *Top of the News* 36 (Winter 1980): 180.

60. Theodore C. Hines and Lois Winkel, "A New Information Access Tool for Children's Media," *Library Resources & Technical Services* 17 (January/March 1983): 94–104.

61. Berman, "Cataloging for Public Libraries," p. 239.

62. Priscilla L. Moulton, "Committee on the Cataloging of Children's Materials: Report," *Library Resources & Technical Services* 13 (Summer 1969): 422.

63. Theodore C. Hines, "Access, Networking, and Children's Services," in *Children & Books,* 6th ed., by Zena Sutherland; Dianne L. Monson; and May Hill Arbuthnot (Glenview, IL: Scott, Foresman, 1981), p. 602.

64. Paul S. Dunkin, *Cataloging U.S.A.* (Chicago: American Library Association, 1969), p. 151.

65. Sara Fine, "Research and the Psychology of Information Use," *Library Trends* 32 (Spring 1984): p. 445.

66. Fine, p. 446.

67. Ruth Gordon, "And Children's Librarians: Some Observations and a Wish List," *The Reference Librarian* 7/8 (Spring/Summer 1983): 94.

68. Donald J. Sager, "Public Library Service to the Microchip Generation," *Top of the News* 39 (Summer 1983): 309.

69. Truett, 1984, p. 274.

70. Robert Bocher, "Mitinet: Catalog Conversion to a MARC Database," *School Library Journal* 31 (March 1985): 109–10.

71. Hines and Winkel, p. 94.

72. Adele M. Fasick, "Moving into the Future without Losing the Past: Children's Services in the Information Age," *Top of the News* 40 (Summer 1984): 407.

73. Ellen M. Markman, "Two Different Kinds of Hierarchical Organization" in *New Trends in Conceptual Representation: Challenge to Piaget's Theory?*, edited by Ellin Kofsky Scholnick (Hillsdale, NJ: Lawrence Erlbaum Associates, Publishers, 1983), p. 183.

74. Dale D. Johnson, "Three Sound Strategies for Vocabulary Development," *Writings in Reading and Language Arts,* Ginn Occasional Papers, no. 3. (Columbus, OH: Ginn, 1982).

75. Berman, "Cataloging for Public Libraries," p. 234.

76. A. C. Foskett, "Better Dead than Read: Further Studies in Critical Classification," *Library Resources & Technical Services* 28 (October/December 1984): 358.

Some Observations Concerning Organization of Serially Published Materials

by Mary Ellen Soper

Everything we collect, organize, and keep in our library collections is either published monographically or serially. These are patterns of publication and do not refer to the format of presentation. A monographically published item in any format is complete in one part or is intended to be complete in a finite number of parts; a serially-published item in any format is issued in parts, which may or may not be numbered, and is intended to continue indefinitely. One or the other of these two patterns of publication describes all the materials we work with and are inherent in our cataloging code.[1] In reality, however, things aren't as simple, so we refer to monographs when we mean books and serials when we mean printed materials published serially. The confusion between format and pattern of publication permeates our terminology and adds to the breakdown in communication between librarians performing different functions. It is doubtful we will ever stop using the term "serial" to mean a particular format, but if we realize its broader, more correct meaning, new formats may not present such a challenge when they appear.

DESCRIPTIVE CATALOGING

Description

Descriptive cataloging, like publishing, separates the description of all items into either "monographic" or "serial." New formats, such as computer software or holograms, and existing formats, like videorecordings, transparencies, maps, and sound recordings, are all first described as monographs or serials, then according to their unique characteristics. In the *Ango-American Cataloguing Rules, 2d edition (AACR2)*, chapters 2–10 deal with all formats published monographically and chapter 12 covers the same formats published serially. Chapter 11, microforms, is used for microreproductions of the formats covered in the other chapters. If an item is determined to be serially published, chapter 12, which emphasizes serially published print materials, should be consulted first for the outline of the description. Then the chapter appropriate to the particular format is consulted for the specific details needed to flesh out the description. The description of format-specific details is not trivial (witness the problems with developing rules for microcomputer software and the intricacies involved with accurately describing music scores and sound recordings), but the problems seem to fall into common patterns, e.g., what to include and what to omit and what area in the eight-area International Standard Bibliographic Description (ISBD) should contain the details. Once the general ISBD pattern is learned, the ISBD for the particular format consulted, the numerous interpretations of the rules and manuals that have appeared since 1978 checked, and local requirements observed, the actual description falls into place rather easily. This sounds complicated, but practice helps to simplify the process.

Serially published materials have special problems. Because serials by definition are meant to continue for an indefinite period, authorship can vary over time. It is difficult for one person to prepare the entire contents of all the parts indefinitely, so authorship is generally spread among many individuals. The result is an example of diffuse authorship, authorship distributed among too many people for any one to be credited with primary responsibility. Although editors can be assumed to control the content, they are not considered to have authored it and therefore are even rejected in most cases from being access points for the publication. As a result, the great majority of serials are entered under their titles (see Exhibit 1 for examples).

There are a few personal author serials, but they are all doomed by the passage of time. A change in authorship is regarded as the same as a change in the title of the serial—a new serial emerges, the old one having ceased publication. In the past, many serials had corporate body authorship, but the problems caused by trying to precisely define corporate authorship led to the exclusion of corporate bodies as authors in most situations.

Since the titles of serials are so important—usually the main point of access—determination of the one, correct title becomes vital. Many librarians still seem most comfortable dealing with monographically published books, where the convention of a title page has been long established. And being monographically published, most books have only one part, hence only one title page. It is necessary to go to only one place to find the correct, unvarying title. But even with the traditional serial format of print serials, determination of title is much more difficult. A title normally appears on the cover, on an interior page close to the front of the issue along with the listing of contents and ownership information, and even possibly in various other places within the issue, such as at the head or foot of pages or on the spine. In addition, an index or table of contents is also published for some print serials when a volume is complete, and a title can be expected there. All these possible locations for the title mean it can vary from place to place in a single issue. It can also vary over time, either intentionally or, as often appears, absentmindedly (see examples 2–5). Each new issue can have a change in title.

The problems caused by this possible multiplicity of titles are two: From what one place in the serial should the title be taken and how can one be certain a title has actually changed? Because of definitions and rule interpretations, the common source of a print serial title is the cover of the first issue (see examples 2–8). A change must then occur within the cover title for a new description to be prepared. The amount of change needed to cause a new description is often quite slight, e.g., a change from an ampersand to the word "and," the change of a preposition from "of" to "for," or vice versa (see examples 4 and 5). Because such a slight change can cause recataloging, the publisher's and editor's integrity (or lack of it) in maintaining the title in a consistent form over time greatly affects the stability of our bibliographic records. The late and much missed *Title Varies* arose as a means for rallying librarians to acquaint publishers with the results of their follies and ask them to desist.[2] It probably didn't accomplish much, but members of Librarians United to Fight Costly, Silly, Unnecessary Serial Title Changes certainly felt better for the effort.

Moving beyond the traditional format of print serials, the titles of other serially published formats can be even more difficult to determine, with even less hope for stability. The print format has existed for many years and the conventions governing its appearance are familiar and accepted by almost everyone. But with nonprint formats the conventions are not so universally accepted, and the publishers and producers are more diverse and often less experienced. Even describing a monographically published nonprint item can be difficult because it is frequently packaged in some kind of container, may be accompanied by printed material, and might even have another format included with it. Thus, there is a possibility of at least three variants of the title. Each chapter in *AACR2* covering the nonprint formats must consider in detail the source of the title and other descriptive information. Even this is inadequate in many cases, so catalogers must often use judgment based on experience or even guesses to settle on a source. When there is uncertainty concerning the source of information, this uncertainty will continue past the point of cataloging and affect the user of the material. The user is forced to try to read the mind of the cataloger, a mind which may have been pretty uncertain at the time. This uncertainty permeating the nonprint formats may be one cause of the discomfort many librarians seem to experience regarding AV materials.

Two results of the uncertainty surrounding many nonprint formats are the appearance of manuals devoted to a single format, such as *Cartographic Materials, Cataloging Machine-Readable Data Files,* and *Graphic Materials,*[3] which explicate pertinent rules, and the need for an organization such as On-Line Audiovisual Catalogers, with its Newsletter,[4] which discusses specific nonprint descriptive problems. When one considers that all formats, print and nonprint, can be published serially, with the resulting possible changes in titles and descriptive elements over time, the uncertainties can multiply almost past imagination. Though serially published nonprint formats are not very common at present, it appears they will increase in the future, since items such as audiocassettes of health sciences journals, videorecordings of TV newscasts, and machine readable serials (the electronic journal) already exist.

Descriptions of serially published items are generally skeletal, omitting holdings information and complete physical details. The information included in area 3—called "Numeric and/or Alphabetic, Chronological, or Other Designation" in chapter 12—pertains to the ideal, the complete run of the title. The actual local holdings in the past have been recorded elsewhere, in files separate from the catalog containing the descriptions. Now, with on-line systems, it is relatively simple to combine the description with the local holdings and finally let our confused users see in one place what material the library really has and in how many physical parts an item exists. How many users in the past, seeing Vol. 1– in a description, and failing to note that they should look elsewhere for actual holdings, have gone to the shelves and been dismayed to see what is actually in the collection?

Another problem with serial descriptions is caused by the reality that many descriptions become inaccurate as time passes. After the first issue of a serially published item has been received and described, the description will generally be left as it is until a title change necessitates the preparation of a new description and the closing off of the old. Many elements of a description—some trivial, some not—could become incorrect as time passes: the publisher, place of publication, other title information, statement of responsibility, size, indexing, variant titles other than the main title, numbering and chronological designations, contents, even frequency. Theoretically, if any of these details changes, the description should be corrected, but it is unlikely that these changes would ever be brought to the attention of the cataloger until the title—or author, if the publication is entered under author—changes. A change in entry should immediately stop the normal processing of newly received issues and generate a review of the whole description. At that time, past changes could be recorded. Because of the possibility that details have become incorrect, most descriptions should be regarded with an informed skepticism. Only when a serially published item ceases publication completely and the description is revised should all the descriptive elements be regarded with some confidence.

Notes can be extensive due to the possibility of change in any element of the description whenever a new issue appears (see example 1). Notes are particularly used to record data that are considered to be especially susceptible to change over time, such as subtitles and editors. Notes also contain the linking information that connects a serially published item with its predecessors, successors, and other manifestations. The rare individual who wants to trace the complete history of an item could follow up on the linking notes and gather together all the previous titles that led to the present situation (see examples 4–5, 8). In an online system, it should be possible for the computer to do all this gathering and present the complete past history of any title together with the current information, once the necessary indexing and connection of links has been done. It is doubtful that most users are interested in such information, or even in much of the other data contained in the description, but extensive details ensure the bibliographic integrity of our files. Also, many librarians believe that our catalogs should be more than finding lists that merely show what items are in a specific collection: they should instead identify the underlying bibliographic works and show relationships between them.

It is probably not necessary for most local library catalogs to contain all the detail required by our rules for descriptive cataloging, but the full bibliographic record needs to be available somewhere so the data will be available for those who need it and for unforeseen future purposes. We once relied primarily on the Library of Congress to produce the bibliographic "records of record" for the country, but now that we have networks such as OCLC, WLN, and RLIN, consisting of large files whose contents include less than half LC-input records, all inputting libraries must take the responsibility for the quality of the database despite the expenses involved. The present descriptive cataloging rules and MARC formats, with their constant changes, additions, and interpretations, are baroque in their complexities. To prepare a full and accurate bibliographic record for a serially published item for input into a database like WLN, which revises records entering it and exercises authority control, is a true experience in persistence and patience. But the result is a record which can be used by everyone for many purposes, a record which should survive for some time.

Entry and Heading

Since there is no longer a specific rule covering the entry of serially published material, several rules have to be considered when entry is determined. Personal authors as main entry are possible, but rare. Entry under corporate body is severely limited by rule 21.1B2. For works with diffuse authorship, and multi-authored works produced under editorial direction, 21.6C2 and 21.7 are the usual rules to consult and will produce a title main entry. But immediately a problem arises with the titles of this material. Since there is no overall "supreme being" controlling titles of any bibliographic material (contents are copyrighted, not titles), there is no way to ensure any one title will be unique. As a result, there was a scramble to develop a rule that would result in unique titles so serially published works could be identified. Eventually, after much backing and filling, 25.5B became the rule for creating a uniform title for any serially published item whose title could be confused with another title. This was done with an extensive and often revised rule interpretation.[5] The rule says a conflict should not be predicted, and the basis for determination of a conflict is the file into which the eventual record is to go. But because records are increasingly shared by many libraries, the real file should be national, or perhaps even international, since countries now exchange bibliographic records. It isn't safe to just look into the local catalog for conflicts; it's now necessary to look much further, even trying to predict conflicts concerning nondistinctive titles. But the difficulty of defining "nondistinctive" led in the past to the plethora of 1949 code rules, the convoluted rule 6 in *AACR2,* and the lengthy rule interpretations of 25.5B in *AACR2.* Experience seems the best guide for determining nondistinctiveness.

Once it has been determined that a uniform title is needed to uniquely identify an item, the uniform title is constructed with a parenthetical modifier. This new title is then attached to the record in main entry position, or, if there is an author, between author and issue title, and from then on becomes the title that identifies the item in catalogs (see examples 6–9). Any listing of serially published materials in a collection will undoubtedly use the uniform title as filing title. We have in effect given the item a new title, separate from that given by the publisher and editor and appearing on the issues themselves. As long as additional access is also provided for the issue title, which will probably be the title appearing in bibliographic citations, our users shouldn't be inconvenienced; surprised, perhaps, if they see our records, but they can still get to the material.

Access in multi-entry files is also commonly provided for any corporate body or person associated with the publication, so the designation of one entry as "main" has little value. The need for *a* main entry is acute, however, in single-entry files. It is also necessary when the publication is cited in another bibliographic record, such as in linking notes or in subject headings and added entries.

Another concern with the uniform title is that the International Standard Serials Number (ISSN) is not linked to it, but instead is linked to the key title, established by the International Serials Data System and its nodes around the world. The key title is shown in area 8 of the ISBN, with the ISSN. The uniform and key titles serve the same function in relation to the item: they both provide a unique identifying title. It is regrettable that two separate systems for creating unique identifiers arose for serially published materials, but it appears we will be burdened with each for a while. Eventually, the uniform and key titles will probably be merged, and the ISSN linked to the result (see examples 6–8 for significant differences between uniform and key titles).

Descriptive cataloging of serially published materials can be regarded as a game, a hunt through luxuriant undergrowth, a gathering in from many places of the necessary details needed to construct an elaborate edifice which may be swept away when the next issue appears. It's a game which should be played seriously, but a chuckle or two is at times appropriate to relieve frustration.

SUBJECT ACCESS

Most attention to providing subject access to serially published materials has been devoted to indexing the contents of print and a few nonprint serials. There are many abstracting and indexing services that cover serials in all languages and subjects. Coverage will be extended to the electronic journals as they become established and generally available. Indexing on the article or microlevel has many features that set it apart from indexing on the serially published item or macrolevel. Online microlevel indexing systems commonly provide many more terms than do macrolevel systems, use postcoordination with descriptors, and may employ uncontrolled vocabulary. If the vocabulary is controlled, typically the relations between terms are much more thoroughly and rigorously specified than in our macrolevel, traditional, library-oriented systems.

The following discussion of subject access will concentrate on the traditional macrolevel systems most widely used in this country: *Library of Congress Classification, Library of Congress Subject Headings,* and the *Dewey Decimal Classification.**

---

*Author's Note: Since this article is appearing in a collection edited by Sanford Berman, little will be said about the Hennepin County Library approach to subject analysis, except that it has much to recommend it, and proves we are shortchanging ourselves by thinking that only the Library of Congress has all the answers. This attitude—that there is no oracle other than LC—is something we've inflicted upon ourselves, and it can't be blamed entirely upon the people in Washington, DC.

Classification

We usually assume that most of our users will approach the contents of our serially published materials through printed or online microlevel indexes. As a result, in many libraries print serials aren't classified; instead they are filed alphabetically by title, separate from the monographically published materials which are arranged in classified order. This is done so the user needn't look up a call number before going to the shelves. Filing by title works as long as the titles are easily determined from the issues and are uncomplicated. Such filing doesn't work as well when the collection is research-oriented or includes many foreign-language journals. Titles in such cases can be difficult to determine and to file accurately. For ease of use, the title on the bound volume and unbound issue should be identical to the one found in the indexes; otherwise, users may have difficulty making a match. Uniform titles would be inappropriate filing titles in such an arrangement. Filing by issue title probably works best for English-language popular periodicals and scholarly journals.

If serially published materials are classified, they could be interfiled with the rest of the collection, thereby permitting maximum serendipity. The problem with such a positive arrangement, however, is that the serial materials by definition are continuing to come and room must be made for the future issues. Growth is not always at a predictable rate. Also, we really don't like messy shelves, and issues waiting for volumes to be complete so they can be bound tend to create mess. As a consequence, a common pattern of arrangement in many larger libraries is to class both serially published and monographically published materials but to keep them in two separate arrangements. An assumption underlying such arrangements appears to be that people who use serials are different from those using monographs, and the two groups have little need to see all materials on a subject available in the collection. We extol the value of serendipity—else why so much effort and expense put into shelf arrangement by classification and open shelving—but do we always appreciate how we restrict serendipity by other things we do?

I happen to believe strongly that nonprint materials, regardless of format, should be treated like print materials, and given the same kind of access. This means physical intershelving, not just interfiling of bibliographic records. As libraries get more serially published nonprint materials, they should at least have the same kind of physical access as the print serials. That they won't is probably true, but we should think more of the ramifications of the decisions we make about shelving than it often appears we do. Restricting physical accessibility results in restricting use, no matter how good the bibliographic access we provide. Even an action as relatively minor as shelving materials below knee level or over six feet above the floor can affect use. Segregating certain materials from the main filing sequence because of format or pattern of publication also limits use artificially. An impressive increase in the use of formerly segregated nonprint formats when they are intershelved into one sequence with more traditional formats has happened consistently in various libraries. Intershelving isn't easy, but it has proven to be quite worth the effort.

The classification of serials is usually simple, particularly since only one class number is regularly assigned in United States libraries. The individual article or part of a run can be quite specific, but the entire run can often be described by a rather broad class number. In the *Dewey Decimal Classification,* the floating Table One contains the standard subdivisions -05 for serial publications and -06 for serial administrative reports and conference proceedings.[6] (See examples 8 and 9 for use of -05 standard subdivisions.) These can be added to almost any class number in volume 2. This would allow a very specific number to be assigned to a serial and the form standard subdivision added to reveal the serial nature; but in practice, assignment often stops at the more generic level.

Dewey classification is much more synthetic than Library of Congress, and therefore has the potential of greater specificity. LC classification lacks the Dewey floating tables and enumerates exactly where serials are to be classed. Serials are generally classed early in the arrangement of topics under a subject, along with other general treatments. For example, HB1-HB846, the schedule for economic theory, classes periodicals/societies/serials in HB1-H9. The merchant marine spans HE730-HE943, its serials classing in HE730.[7] Even where tables are used, such as for individual philosophers in class B, there is an enumerated place in each table for the serials about the philosophers. This place isn't always at the start of the sequence, but a slot *does* exist, whether needed for a particular person or not.[8]

This last observation is of interest, since LC classification is supposed to be governed by literary warrant: class numbers aren't created until material exists to warrant their creation. But there are places where common patterns are listed, such as in the many tables where class numbers exist that may have no potential use. Dewey classification, with its extensive synthetic elements, has many more such non-useful class numbers.

The value of classification in bringing together materials on the same and related subjects is tempered by the reality that both Dewey and LC classifications are disciplined-based, with specific subjects scattered throughout the disciplines, depending upon the approach to the subject being taken in each case. Librarians should be familiar with this—since it's drilled into them in beginning cataloging classes—though they sometimes seem to forget it when they question why certain materials are classed where they are. For example: a print serial on television usually goes in recreational and performing arts, but if it deals with TV as a teaching aid, it belongs in education and TV as a news medium should be in journalism, while TV technology belongs in electronic and communication engineering.

Subject Headings

Unlike classification numbers, more than one subject heading can be assigned to a given item. In practice, rarely are more than one or two subject headings assigned to serially published materials, because the level of analysis, similar to classification, is not very extensive. The generality of the subject headings usually matches the generality of the class number. The form subdivision PERIODICALS is most commonly used, and, since it is free-floating, can be added after topical or geographic subject headings for all regularly published serials[9] (see examples 1–9). This subdivision, along with AB-STRACTS--PERIODICALS; COLLECTED WORKS; CONGRESSES; DIRECTORIES; INDEXES; SOCIETIES, ETC.; SOCIETIES, PERIODICALS, ETC. (used with personal names); and YEAR-BOOKS is employed in the same way the Dewey -05 and -06 standard subdivisions are used: they denote the subject presented in a particular pattern of publication or format. Such use of form subdivisions is also common with nonprint materials. The lack of use of a form subdivision with monographically published print materials could be regarded as a sign of general conviction that such material is the standard type of library material and all other types are "different" and in need of being so designated. The use of general material designators (GMDs) in the description also supports this interpretation; GMDs are available for all formats covered by *AACR2*, but LC doesn't use all of them. The GMD for monographically published print materials—text—is one of the major exclusions in the use of GMDs.

Subject heading lists could be assumed to contain only terms that indicate the subject content of materials, but they also contain terms that describe form rather than subject. Sometimes scope notes point out the correct usage: ESSAY is the subject heading, ESSAYS the form heading. Sometimes usage can be inferred by a scope note under one heading, but omitted from the other: CONCERTO is the subject heading, CONCERTOS (and all its offshoots) the form heading.[10] The headings used with serially published materials are almost all subject headings, though few have the scope notes saying so. According to Chan, almost all headings that describe bibliographic forms are in fact subject or topical headings, not form headings,[11] though the Library of Congress could change usage in the future.

A quick search through the ninth edition of *Library of Congress Subject Headings* garnered the following representative list of headings:

ALMANACS
AMERICAN NEWSPAPERS (illustrates pattern to be followed
    for other languages or areas)
AMERICAN PERIODICALS (illustrates pattern to be followed
    for other languages or areas)
BLIND, PERIODICALS FOR THE
CHILDRENS' PERIODICALS
CHILDRENS' PERIODICALS, FRENCH (illustrates pattern to
    be followed for other languages and areas)
COLLEGE AND SCHOOL PERIODICALS
DEAF, PERIODICALS FOR THE
FANZINES
LITTLE MAGAZINES
MONOGRAPHIC SERIES
NEWSLETTERS
NEWSPAPERS
PERIODICALS
POLYGLOT PERIODICALS
PRISON PERIODICALS
SCHOLARLY PERIODICALS
SERIAL PUBLICATIONS
SERIES (PUBLICATIONS)
WOMEN'S PERIODICALS
YEARBOOKS

Only NEWSPAPERS and PERIODICALS are clearly designated as just subject headings, but most of the rest are clearly not to be used as form headings. ALMANACS and YEARBOOKS can be used for both the topic and the form. The approach to serially published materials on specific subjects is through the [topic]--[subdivision] construction, using one of the appropriate form subdivisions. According to LC, serially published materials with very general contents are not to be assigned form headings, even when there is a desire to bring together material in a specific language or from a specific country. AMERICAN PERIODICALS and similar headings strictly denote topics, not forms.

There is, however, often a need felt in libraries to bring together in one place materials in certain languages or from certain areas, or even in certain broad subjects, resulting in an overpowering desire to assign such headings as BRAZILIAN PERIODICALS or RUSSIAN PERIODICALS to materials in all subjects, POLITICAL PERIODI-

CALS instead of LC's POLITICAL SCIENCE--PERIODICALS, and HISTORICAL PERIODICALS instead of LC's HISTORY--PERIODICALS. As long as such usages are restricted to a local library, and help local users, there is no reason such headings shouldn't be used, although users do travel and may wonder why such headings aren't available in other libraries. The local library will have to note this nonstandard usage carefully to achieve consistency.

A problem arises in networks containing records contributed by many libraries. Network standards usually dictate what rules are to be followed. Nonstandard usages can cause problems if they creep in. In WLN, which has record review and authority control, the network staff periodically has to remind member libraries that nonstandard usages of LC subject headings are not allowed, and they are not to be input. The presence of such topical headings as AMERICAN PERIODICALS, with no scope note clearly stating they cannot be used as form headings, leads easily to misinterpretation and hence misuse. If LC would increase the number of scope notes to cover situations where topics and forms are identical, the misuse should decrease, but it is unlikely to do this. If the networks would index the language field in the MARC records, and thus make it searchable, the pressure to assign headings indicating language would probably lessen considerably. In the meantime, a cautious approach to the assignment of subject headings is called for; on the surface, subject headings appear simple, but they are full of traps for the unwary.

Bibliographic control of serially published materials has many problems, some of which are unique to the pattern of publication. Because serials continue to be issued, they are subject to changes with each new issue, which may or may not affect the description and subject analysis. Librarians who have to handle serials daily either switch jobs quickly or develop a perverse pride in their wayward charges. They even have adopted a name for themselves— serialists—which helps to set them apart and increases their feeling of kinship with others with similiar perversions. Some futurists predict print formats are dying, to be replaced with electronic media. Whether they are right or wrong, the pattern of publication of serials seems certain to continue, regardless of format, promising continual aggravation, joy, and jobs for confirmed serialists.

EXHIBIT 1
Examples

The following examples were suggested by *LC and AACR2: an album of cataloging examples arranged by rule number* / Alan M. Greenberg, Carole R. McIver.—Metuchen, N.J.: Scarecrow Press, 1984 (citation in ISBD format). The actual examples were printed out in full display from the WLN database in April 1985. WLN includes the key title in its complete display of MARC tagging, but omits it from the full display; therefore, the key title is shown at the bottom of the examples if one has been included in the record.

Example 1

```
      Bibliografia ecuatoriana = Ecuadorian bibliography / Biblioteca
General de la Universidad Central del Ecuador. No. 1 (enero/feb.
1975)- Quito : La Biblioteca, c1975-
      v. ; 22 cm.
      Semiannual (irregular), 1976-<1978>
      Numbers 6-<8-9> dropped parallel titles.
      Some issues are cumulations with title: Anuario bibliografico
ecuatoriano.
      Other title:  Anuario bibliografico ecuatoriano
      Cover title:  Anuario bibliografico ecuatoriano y bibliografia
ecuatoriana no. 6, 8-9-
      Issues for Jan./Feb.-Sept./Oct. 1975 called also ano 1.
      1. Ecuador--Imprints--Periodicals. I. Universidad Central del
Ecuador. Biblioteca General. II. Title: Ecuadorian bibliography
III.  Title: Anuario bibliografico ecuatoriano y bibliografia
ecuatoriana no. 6, 8-9-
      Z1761 .B52       015/.866 19
      PPT    77-649113  //r83
```

Shows two variant titles and a parallel title. Also shows variation in frequency and numbering.

Example 2

```
      Micro systems. Vol. 1, no. 1 (Jan./Feb. 1980)-v. 1, no. 2
(Mar./Apr. 1980). [Mountainside, NJ : Libes, c1980]
      1 v. : ill. ; 28 cm.
      Six no. a year
      Title from cover.
      At head of title, Jan./Apr. 1980: "S-100."
      Running title:  S-100 microsystems
      Continued by:  Microsystems 0199-7955
      ISSN  0199-7955 0274-6921
      1. Microcomputers--Periodicals. 2. Minicomputers--Periodicals.
   I.  Title: S.-one hundred microsystems II. Title:  S-100
microsystems
      QA76.6 .M515       001.64 19
      NSDP    82-646521
```

Key title = Microsystems

Example 3

```
     Microsystems. Vol. 1, no. 3 (May/June 1980)-v. 5, no. 11 (Nov.
1984). [Springfield, N.J. : Libes, c1980-1984.
     5 v. : ill. ; 28 cm.
     Monthly <, Mar. 1983- >
     Title from cover.
     Running title:  S-100 microsystems
     Continues:  Micro systems 0199-7955
     Indexed in its entirety by:  Computer & control abstracts
0036-8113 July/Aug. 1982-
     Indexed in its entirety by:  Electrical & electronics abstracts
0036-8105 July/Aug. 1982-
     Indexed in its entirety by: Physics abstracts. Science abstracts.
Series A 0036-8091 July/Aug. 1982-
     Indexed selectively by: Predicasts
     ISSN  0199-7955
     1. Microcomputers--Periodicals.  2. Microcomputers--
Programming--Periodicals. I. Title: S.-one hundred microsystems II.
Title: S-100 microsystems
     QA76.6 .M515         001.64 19
     TxU     82-646380
```

Key title = Microsystems

A minor change in title after first two issues required a new description. Also shows cover used as source of title, one variant title, and a change in place of publication. Abstracting and indexing services are listed in separate notes of the second description. Key title differs slightly from title in first description.

Example 4

```
     5 year highway construction & airport development program.
-Fiscal year 1980. [Phoenix] : Arizona Dept. of Transportation,
-1980].
     v. : ill. ; 22 x 28 cm.
     Annual
     Description based on: Fiscal year 1980; title from cover.
     Continues: 5 year construction program, highways and airports
     Continued by: 5 year highway construction and airport development
program 1980/81-
     Report year ends June 30.
     Began with 1979.
     1. Highway planning--Arizona--Periodicals.  2. Airports--
Arizona--Planning--Periodicals.  I. Arizona. Dept. of
Transportation. II. Title: Five year construction & airport
development program III. Title: 5 year highway construction and
airport development program
     HE356.A7 A15         388.1/09791
     DDOT     82-642525
```

Example 5

Change from ampersand to "and" in title required new description (below). Cover used as source of title. First description shows former and later titles; second shows former title.

```
       5 year highway construction and airport development program.
Fiscal year 1981- [Phoenix] : Arizona Dept. of Transportation,
[1981-
       v. : ill. ; 22 x 28 cm.
       Annual
       Title from cover.
       Continues: 5 year highway construction & airport development
program
       Report year ends June 30.
          1. Highway planning--Arizona--Periodicals. 2.  Airports--
Arizona--Planning--Periodicals. I. Arizona. Dept. of
Transportation. II. Title: Five year highway construction and
airport development program
       HE356.A7 A15        388.1/09791
          82-642526
```

Example 6

```
       Industrial wastes (Chicago, Ill. : 1971)
       Industrial wastes. [Des Plaines, Ill. : Scranton Gillette
Communications, Inc.,
              v.
       Bimonthly
       Description based on: Vol. 28, no. 3 (May/June 1982); title
from cover.
       Previously published as a separately paginated section in:
Water & sewage works.
       Began in 1971.
       Indexed in its entirety by: Applied science & technology index
0003-6986
       Indexed selectively by: Engineering index monthly (1984)
0742-1974
       Indexed selectively by: Engineering index bioengineering
abstracts 0736-6213
       Indexed selectively by: Engineering index energy abstracts
0093-8408
       Indexed selectively by: Excerpta medica
       Indexed selectively by: Selected water resources abstracts
0037-136X
       Indexed selectively by: Coal abstracts 0309-4979
       Indexed selectively by: Energy information abstracts 0147-6521
       Indexed selectively by: Environment abstracts 0093-3287
       Indexed selectively by: Chemical abstracts 0009-2258
       Indexed selectively by: Energy research abstracts Sept.
1975- 0160-3604
       Indexed selectively by: Engineering index annual (1968)
0360-8557
       ISSN  0046-9262
          1. Factory and trade waste--Periodicals.
       TD896 .I64        628.4 19
       NSDP    82-646131
```

Key title = Industrial wastes (1971)

Extensive notes, many of which are a result of the project to add to serial records all the abstracting and indexing services that cover or selectively cover the particular title. Key title differs significantly from uniform title. Cover is source of title.

Example 7

```
     Public affairs review (Public Affairs Council)
     Public affairs review : journal of the Public Affairs Council.
[Washington, D.C.] : The Council,
     v. ; 23 cm.
     Annual
     Description based on: Vol. 2 (1981); title from cover.
     Began with vol. for 1980.
     ISSN 0276-0843
     1. Business and politics--United States--Periodicals. I.
Public Affairs Council.
     JK467 .P83         322/.3/0973
     NSDP     81-642764
```

Key title = Public affairs review (Washington, DC)

Uniform title created as main entry differs significantly from key title. Cover is source of title.

Example 8

```
     AD (London, England : 1969)
     AD. [Vol. 39, 7] (7/1969)-Apr. 1970. [London : Standard
Catalogue Co., 1969-1970].
     2 v. : ill. ; 28-32 cm.
     Monthly
     Title from cover.
     Continues: Architectural design (London, England : 1949)
0003-8504
     Continued by: A.D. (London, England : 1970) 0003-8504 1970
     Vol. numbering ceases with Dec. 1969.
     Indexed selectively by: Architectural periodicals index
0033-6912 July 1969-Apr. 1970
     ISSN 0003-8504
     1. Architecture--Periodicals. I. Title: A.D.
     NA1 .A563        720/.5
        75-642284  //r82
```

Key title = Architectural design

Uniform title differs significantly from key title. Key title and ISSN should have been changed when title proper changed. Two title changes shown in notes. Cover is source of title.

Example 9

Uniform title created for nondistinctive title. Key title differs in punctuation. Ceased date not shown in body of record, but only in a note (below).

```
      Circular (Virginia Geological Survey)
      Circular / Commonwealth of Virginia, Virginia Conservation
Commission, Virginia Geological Survey. 1- University, Va. : The
Survey, 1941-
      6 v. : ill. ; 23 cm.
      Irregular
      No. 1-   prepared in cooperation with the U.S. Geological
Survey.
      Has occasional supplements.
      Ceased with 6 (1947).
      ISSN 0733-0782
      1. Geology--Virginia--Periodicals. I. Virginia Geological
Survey. II. Geological Survey (U.S.)
      QE173 .A38        557.55/05 19
      MUL    42-036667   //r822
```

Key title = Circular - Virginia Geological Survey

REFERENCES

1. *Anglo-American Cataloging Rules,* 2d ed. (Chicago: American Library Association, 1978), Appendix D: Glossary - Monographs, p. 568; Serials, p. 570.

2. *Title Varies,* 1 (1) (December 1973) and 6 (3–5) (December 1980). Librarians United to Fight Costly, Silly Unnecessary Serial Title Changes; founding father, David Taylor.

3. *Cartographic Materials: a Manual of Interpretation for AACR2.* Prepared by the Anglo-American Cataloguing Committee for Cartographic Materials. (Chicago: American Library Association, 1982); Dodd, Sue A. *Cataloging Machine-Readable Data Files: an Interpretive Manual.* (Chicago: American Library Association, 1982); Betz, Elisabeth W. *Graphic Materials: Rules for Describing Original Items and Historical Collections* (Washington, DC: Library of Congress, 1982).

4. On-Line Audiovisual Catalogers, *Newsletter* 1 (1) (January 1981–) (Lake Crystal, MN: OLAC, 1981–).

5. *Library of Congress Rule Interpretations for AACR2: a Cumulation from Cataloging Service Bulletin Number 11-.* (Oberlin, OH: Oberlin College Library, 1982–), p. 142 (revised 11/84).

6. Dewey, Melvil. *Dewey Decimal Classification and Relative Index,* 19th ed. (Albany, NY: Forest Press, 1979), vol. 1, table 1, p. 6.

7. *Library of Congress Classification.* Class H: Subclasses H-HJ, 4th ed. (Washington, DC: Library of Congress, 1981), p. 10, 137.

8. *Library of Congress Classification.* Class B: Subclasses B-BJ, 3d ed. (Washington, DC: Library of Congress, 1979), p. 105–09.

9. Library of Congress, Subject Cataloging Division. *Library of Congress Subject Headings: a Guide to Subdivision Practice.* (Washington, DC: Library of Congress, 1981), p. 54.

10. Library of Congress, Subject Cataloging Division. *Library of Congress Subject Headings.* 9th ed. (Washington, DC: Library of Congress, 1980).

11. Chan, Lois Mai. *Library of Congress Subject Headings: Principles and Application.* Littleton, CO: Libraries Unlimited, 1978), p. 59.

Fine Arts

by R. Cecilia Knight

This paper considers some of the idiosyncrasies in cataloging fine arts monographs.

It provides an overview and reference on fine arts cataloging practices. These practices represent an attempt at consistency in access and description of the body of information of and about the fine arts.

The perimeters of fine arts will be defined to include the subjects in the N (Fine Arts) schedules of the Library of Congress Classification plus TR (Photography), and in Dewey Decimal classes 700–709 and 720–779.

DDC		LC	
700	The Arts	N	Visual Arts (General)
720	Architecture	NA	Architecture
730	Plastic Arts Sculpture	NB	Sculpture
740	Drawing, decorative and minor arts	NC	Drawing Design Illustration
750	Painting and Paintings	ND	Painting
760	Graphic arts Prints	NE	Print media
		NK	Decorative arts, applied arts Decoration and ornament

DDC	LC
	NX Arts in general
770 Photography and Photographs	TR Photography

(Not all of the examples used here will be classified in these areas, particularly some of the items about places.)

As can be seen in this brief comparison, these two systems are very similar, with the Library of Congress scheme being based on DDC's arrangement for the arts.

In a way, this similarity is disconcerting. It means that in Dewey and LC alike, individual artists will be classified in several different places, as shown in the examples below, unless they manage to channel all of their creative energies through one artistic format.

This makes each new work an adventure in classification.

McMullen, Roy. *Degas: his life, times, and work.*
(This work discusses Degas as a painter)

ND	Painting	759.4	French Artists
200	Special countries		
+353	France-Special Artists		
553			
D298	A-Z (for Degas)	D317	Cutter (for Degas)
*M38	Author	M168	Author

Dunlop, Ian, 1940– *Degas.* (This is a biography treating his work in painting, drawing, sculpture, etc.)

N	Visual arts	709.24	Art, general-Artist
6500	Special countries		
+353	France-Special Artists		
6853			
D33	A-Z (for Degas)	D317	Cutter (for Degas)
*D4	Biography (by ed.)	D922	Local provision may be made to double Cutter

Breakdown under an artist

.x	Cutter for individual
.xA2-29	Autobiography (by title)
.xA3-34	Letters (by title)
.xA35-39	Miscellaneous. Speeches, essays, etc. (by title)
.xA4-59	Reproductions cataloged under artist's name when there is no editor (by title)
.xA6-Z	Reproductions (by editor); catalogs (by editor or corporate body responsible for preparation); biography and criticism (by main entry); title entries (by title); etc.

Four tables in the N schedules provide breakdown by geographic area, chronology, and special artists. There are also special provisions within the schedules indicated by "Divide like" notes. These are straightforward and do not pose a problem to anyone familiar with LC classification.

Dewey, though less exhaustive, works on the same principles. The individual artist is brought out under his or her country (unless the library chooses the option for 7X0.92) and a double cutter is assigned: first for the artist, then for the author, etc. following local decision for cuttering procedures.

Again, like LC, there are interior provisions for repeating divisions that are useful under several forms, e.g., 704.942–.949 for subjects in art. The divisions after the decimal point (.942–.949) may also be used after 779.X for subjects in photographs.

A more basic difficulty faced in the classification of "pictorial works" is determining whether they are art books or something else. One factor to look at is whether or not the people responsible for the visual matter are artists. This can usually be determined by reading the introductory text to see if there is any mention of artistic technique, interpretation, or meaning, or whether the work essentially contains representations of items for botanical, historical, or other purposes.

Two monographs consisting almost entirely of photographic reproductions with the subject heading ARIZONA--DESCRIPTION AND TRAVEL--VIEWS will be classed in two different locations (TR-photography and F-history in LC or the 770s-photography and 970s-history in DDC) because one is by Edward Weston (an artist) and the other issued to promote tourism. Other examples of this may be found under the subject heading FLOWERS IN ART: Anderson, Frank J. *An illustrated treasury of cultivated flowers.* (SB407.A54 or 635.90222.A546); Meyerowitz, Joel. *Wild flowers: photographs.*

(TR654.M46385 or 779.0924.M613); Davids, Arlette. *Rock plants/ drawn by. . .*(N7680.D28 or 758.42.D251).

CHOICE OF ENTRY

For the majority of monographs in the fine arts, choice of entry under *AACR2* is the same as for any other discipline. However, in the arts there are situations that occur on a regular basis—particularly when the title page is complicated or incomplete—that require corporate entries and partial or variant title added entries to enhance access.

Frequently a book of an artist's works will be titled [Name of artist]: [descriptive subtitle] and the work will consist almost entirely of reproductions of the artist's work accompanied by a brief introductory text by one or more people. In such a case, the artist receives both a main and a subject entry; the subtitle receives a partial title added entry; and "predominantly named" persons and/or corporate bodies associated with the compilation and/or text of the work receive added entries.

```
        Picasso, Pablo, 1881-1973 Pablo Picasso : the last ten years /
    edited by William Brown ; chronology by James H. White.
        Note: Organized by the Museum of Modern Art, New York with the
    collaboration of the Reunion des musees nationaux de France.

        1. Picasso, Pablo, 1881-1973. I. Brown, William. II. White,
    James H. III. Museum of Modern Art (New York, N.Y.) IV. Reunion des
    musees nationaux (France) V. Title: Last ten years.

        Cartier-Bresson, Henri, 1908- Henri Cartier-Bresson : carnet
    de notes sur le Mexique.

        1. Mexico City (Mexico)--Description--Views. 2.
    Photography--Exhibitions. 3. Cartier-Bresson, Henri, 1908- I.
    Title: Carnet de notes sur le Mexique.
```

Art catalogs and exhibition catalogs which contain reproductions or reproductions and texts are entered under the person who wrote the catalog if she or he is represented as the author. If not, entry is under the artist's name. For catalogs that do not contain reproductions, enter (1) under the author, (2) under the title, or (3) if a corporate body or individual owns all of the works listed and also issued the catalog, under that body or individual.

The times when an exhibition catalog or the catalog of a collection should receive corporate main entry are narrowly defined. As mentioned in the previous paragraph, and demonstrated in the third (Musee Picasso) and fourth (Escuela Nacional) examples (below), the rule is: ownership of the items plus the catalog must emanate from the corporate body.

Added entries are not made under every museum and gallery associated with an art book. If the corporate body's function is

```
     Fairweather, Sally H.,1917- Picasso's concrete sculptures /
by...

     1. Picasso, Pablo, 1881-1973--Catalogs. I. Picasso, Pablo,
1881-1973.

     Picasso, Pablo, 1881-1973. L'uvre de Picasso `a Antibes,
Antibes : Musee Picasso, 1981.

     1. Picasso, Pablo, 1881-1973. 2. Musee Picasso (Antibes,
France)--Exhibitions. I. Musee Picasso (Antibes, France)

     Musee Picasso. Picasso's Picassos : a catalog from the Musee
Picasso, Paris / selected by Sir Roland Penrose...[et al.]

     1. Picasso, Pablo, 1881-1973--Catalogs. 2. Musee Picasso (Paris,
France)--Catalogs. I. Picasso, Pablo, 1881-1973. II. Penrose, Roland,
Sir.



     Escuela Nacional de Bellas Artes (Mexico) La escultura del siglo
XIX : catalogo de colecciones de la Escuela Nacional de Bellas Artes,
(Published for the Escuela Nacional by the Instituto Nacional de Bellas
Artes.)
```

limited to publication and/or distribution, no added entry would be made. If its contributions to the work are more extensive (i.e., supplying the staff and/or finances), or if such statements as "organized by" or "in association with" appear on the item, an added entry may be made. If the cataloger feels that corporate access is necessary (due to local interest or special collections) and a corporate added entry cannot be made under 21.30E of *AACR2,* a subject cntry might be appropriate.

When each of the locations where a show will be exhibited is listed on the title page along with the dates it will appear in each place, give this information in either "other title" information or in a note. Unless a museum or gallery has more responsibility for the show than simply housing it (i.e., owning or organizing it), no added entry will be made for these corporate bodies.

Exhibitions (see examples below) are treated under 21.1B1-2 of *AACR2* and there are very few which can be established as named corporate bodies under 21.1B1 due to the requirements of appellation (versus general description), consistency, and capitalization. Some exhibitions may be entered under the sponsoring/owning corporate body using the criteria discussed in the previous paragraphs.

An in-depth study of 21.1B1-2 and related rule interpretations will help in making these determinations. In all cases, added entries are made for all prominently named persons and corporate bodies within the limitations used for all types of materials under *AACR2.*

Wright, Frank Lloyd, 1867-1959. <u>Frank Lloyd Wright, drawing,</u>
<u>1887-1959 : Napoli, Palazzo Reale, 9 December 1976-10 January 1977;</u>
<u>Paris, Ecole speciale d'architecture, 4 June-9 July 1977;</u>
<u>Helsinki, Museum of Finnish Architecture, 10 August-10 September</u>
<u>1977; Wien, Kunsterhaus, 7-27 November 1977.</u>
Note: Catalogue of an exhibition organized by the University of Naples
Institute of Architectural Analysis in collaboration with the Frank
Lloyd Wright Memorial Foundation, Taliesin, Ariz.

   I. Universita di Napoli. Istituto di analisi architettonica. II.
Frank Lloyd Wright Foundation.

   <u>From the Suntory Museum of art : autumn grasses and water...</u>
Published: New York : Japan Society, 1983.
Note: "Catalogue of an exhibition shown at Japan House Gallery in the
Fall of 1983 and organized by Japan Society and Tokyo's Suntory Museum
of Art."

   I. Suntory Bijutsukan. II. Japan Society (New York, N.Y.)

PUBLICATION

Most of the time, the big, beautiful art books are issued by major publishing companies and there is no question as to when, where, and by whom an item was published. At times, however, other types of art books are rather vague about who published them or *if* they were published.

For privately printed items such as artists' books and catalogs, consider the publisher to be whoever issued the item—whether a commercial publisher, private press (if nothing indicates differently), or person or group for whom it was printed. If no publisher is named and there is a copyright holder, consider the copyright holder to be the publisher. If no publisher is named, but a corporate body is cited at the head of the title, assume that the body is the publisher unless other indications signal that it is not (See *AACR2* 1.4 and 2.4 and *LC Rule Interpretations* for further information.)

PHYSICAL DESCRIPTION

Physical description under *AACR2* is fairly easy. Art materials frequently require the use of the phrases "ill." and "chiefly ill., (some col.)." Rule 2.5C, *Illustrative matter,* defines which terms may be used and how they should be used.

ill.   is used for all illustrations other than those
             provided for by a specific term.

col. ill.   is used for works with color illustrations.

ill. (some col.)	is used when only some of the illustrations are color: "(some col.)" may be appended to all of the terms excepting "col. ill."
chiefly ill.	for a work made up predominantly of illustrations with very little accompanying text.
all ill.	for a work made up completely of illustrations: "all" may also be used with "col. ill.," "maps," etc.
maps, map	for maps.
ports., port.	for portraits.
charts	for charts.
coats of arms	for coats of arms of families, royal houses, etc.
facsims., facsim.	for facsimiles.
forms	when forms or examples of forms are included.
geneal. tables	for genealogical tables.
music	for written music.
plans	for architectural plans, etc.

These are arranged alphabetically in the physical description field, except for "ill." which appears first whenever used.

58 p.: chiefly ill. (some col.); Examples: 20 cm.
22 p.: all col. ill.; 20 cm.
48 p.: ill., ports.; 29 cm.
620 p., 20 leaves of plates: ill. (some col.), ports.; 24 cm.
139 p., 1 folded leaf of plates : ill.; 29 cm.
63 p. [77] p. of plates : ill. (some col.) ; 31 cm.
vii, 256 p.: col. ill.; 28 cm.
113 p.: chiefly col. ill. ; 28 cm.

119 p.: chiefly ill. (some col.) ; 35 cm.
272 p., [61] leaves of plates : ill., maps; 26 cm.
128 p.: ports. ; 29 cm.

NOTES

The use of notes in arts cataloging offers great possibilities. The items are often published in limited quantities by individuals or by small presses. There are frequently title variants, other title information, signatures, and interesting embellishments. Below are some examples of unusual types of notes that may be necessary to accurately describe a monograph in the fine arts.

Title:
  Title from portfolio.
  Cataloged from portfolio.
Variant titles:
  On inside front flap: The little red book.
  Title on frontispiece: Hommage a Raphael.
Parallel titles and other title information:
  Parallel title in picture writing using the international symbol
    for "no" over a bowl of fruit.
  Place and dates of exhibition from verso of t.p.
Responsibility:
  "Catalogue compiled by Jane Anderson and Stuart Nelson."—T.p. verso.
  Signed: N.C. Bennett.
  "Exhibition organized by the Friends of Geometric Sequences."—Colophon.
Edition and history:
  "This book is an edition of 1,000."—T.p. verso.
  "Published in an edition of 75 copies."
  Five hundred copies.
  "Limited to 15 copies signed by the artist."
  "Edition of 450 numbered copies."
  "Printed by the artist."
  "Privately printed by Michael Edwards."
Physical description:
  Accompanied by slides of the exhibition inserted in pocket
    in back.
  Miniature music box which plays 'Love me tender' between
    pages 52 and 53.
Copy specific notes:
  Library has copy 2 of 5.

"No. 26 [signed] Joe Ruther."—T.p.
"[Two hundred] copies have been printed. . .this is no. 112."
Other notes:
> Photographers: Ellen Brooks, Eileen Cowin, Jimmy De Sana, Barbara Kruger, Sherrie Levine, Richard Prince, Don Rodan, Cindy Sherman, Laurie Simmons.
>
> "Catalogue of the exhibition held June 7–15 1984 at the Center for Creative Photography, Tucson, Ariz."
>
> Catalog of an exhibition held December 12 1975–January 15 1976.
>
> "Published in connection with the exhibition. . .presented at the Detroit Institute of Art, August 11–November 1, 1981; the Art Institute of Chicago, January 15–March 8, 1982."—T.p. verso.

SUBJECT HEADINGS

Applying *Library of Congress Subject Headings* is a challenge in any discipline. The arts are no exception. A general outline of the types of headings that might be necessary and applicable for the most common types of art books follows:

Monographs created as works of art
1. Artists' books.
2. [Name of artist]
3. [Topic] (when appropriate).

Example
1. Artists' books. 2. Anderson, Harry. 3. Photography, Artistic.

Single artist

About his/her work:
1. [Name of artist]
2. [Form] (when appropriate).

Example
1. Warhol, Andy, 1928– 2. Painting, Modern.

Biography
1. [Name of artist]
2. [Type]--[Biographical subdivision], e.g.:
   Painters--Biography.
   --Interviews.
   --Correspondence.
   --Homes and haunts.

Example
   1. Wright, Frank Lloyd, 1867–1959. 2. Architects--United States-
-Interviews.

Exhibitions and catalogs
   1. [Name of artist]
   2. [Name of Museum]--Exhibitions.
      --Catalogs.
   3. [Topic]--Exhibitions.
      --Catalogs.
   4. [Form]--Exhibitions. (as appropriate)
      --Catalogs.

Example
   1. Degas, Edgar, 1834–1917. 2. Dancers in art--Exhibitions. 3.
Art Institute of Chicago--Exhibitions.

**Catalogs of art collections (for exhibition catalogs, use the subdivision
--Exhibitions)**

Unnamed
   1. [Form]--Catalogs. (as appropriate)
      --Exhibitions.
   2. [Form]--[Place collection is located]--Catalogs.
      --Exhibitions.
   3. [Museum]--Catalogs.
      --Exhibitions.

Example
   1. Painting--Catalogs. 2. Painting--France--Paris--Catalogs. 3.
Musee du Louvre--Catalogs.

Named
   1. [Form]--Catalogs. (as appropriate)
      --Exhibitions.
   2. [Form]--[Place collection is located]--Catalogs.
      --Exhibitions.
   3. [Name of collection]--Catalogs.
      --Exhibitions.
   4. [Museum]--Catalogs
      --Exhibitions.

Example
   1. Painting, French--Exhibitions. 2. Painting, Modern--Chi-
cago--Catalogs. 3. Williams Collection--Exhibitions. 4. Art Institute of
Chicago--Exhibitions.

Private collections

Individual owner (exhibitions and catalogs):
1. [Form]--Exhibitions. (as appropriate)
   --Catalogs.
2. [Name of original owner]--Art collections--Exhibitions.
   --Catalogs.
3. [Form]--Private Collections (Indirect)--Exhibitions.
   --Catalogs.

Example
1. Sculpture--Catalogs. 2. De Rothchild, J. A. (James Armand), 1878–1957--Art collections--Catalogs. 3. Sculpture--Private collections--Great Britain--Catalogs.

Belonging to more than one person

Family
1. [Form]--Private collections (Indirect)
2. [Family name]--Art collections.
3. [Name of prominently named family member]--Art collections.
   (if appropriate)

Example
1. Prints, Indian--Private collections--Maryland--Baltimore. 2. Walsh family--Art collections. 3. Walsh, Eleanore Jane, 1912- --Art collections.

Husband and wife
1. [Form]--Private collections (Indirect)
2. [First named spouse]--Art collections.
3. [2nd named spouse]--Art collections. (unless the couple is referred to as Mr. and Mrs. John X., make the heading only for the person whose name is easily determined).

Example
1. Painting, Dutch--Private collections. 2. Painting, Modern--Netherlands--Exhibitions. 3. Carter, Edward William, 1911- --Art Collections. [Mr. and Mrs. "Edward William Carter" on piece]

Exhibitions not covered above under artist or collections
1. [Form]--Exhibitions. (as appropriate)
2. [Name of museum that owns the items]--Exhibitions.

Example
1. Impressionism (art)--Exhibitions. 2. Art Institute of Chicago--Exhibitions.
Note: [Form] can mean:
Painting.
Painting, French (Indirect)--History.
Painting, Modern (Indirect) (Style also denotes chronology).

Painting, Islamic (Indirect)--History.
Cubism.
Prairie school (Architecture).
Abstract expressionism.
Art deco.
etc.

(More than one may be necessary to bring out the topic.)

The various fine art forms—painting, sculpture, etc.—are modified by national, ethnic, or religious qualifiers as well as "Indirectly." Most of the decorative art forms are not as versatile and take only style, ethnic, and religious qualifiers. Always check the LC Subject Heading list for options.

Buildings
1. [Name of building] (Geographic qualifier)--[Name of detail]
   --[Name of part of building]
2. [Name of architect]
3. [City]--[Type of building]
4. [Name of owner or resident]--Homes (Indirect)
   --Homes and haunts (Indirect)

Example
1. Paul R. Hanna House (Stanford, Calif.) 2. Wright, Frank Lloyd, 1867–1959. 3. Usonian houses--California--Stanford. 4. Hanna, Paul Robert, 1902--Homes.

Work of art
1. [Name of artist]//[Title of work] if artist is not known:
1. [Title of work]

Example
1. Picasso, Pablo, 1881–1973.//Guernica.

(The original work would have the artist as the main entry, the title of the work would have an added entry, and subject headings would be assigned for the subject content of the work.)

Subdivisions

In addition to these patterns for subject analysis, a condensed list of commonly used subdivisions, including a few examples and notes to define their scope, may be useful. These are excerpted from the Library of Congress Subject Cataloging Division's *Subject Cataloging Manual: Subject Headings (1984)* and the *Library of Congress Subject Headings: a Guide to Subdivision Practice (1981):*

Art	Use under names of individuals who lived before 1400 and legendary figures, e.g.,

MARY, VIRGIN--ART
For real persons after 1400, see PORTRAITS, ETC.; PORTRAITS, CARICATURES, ETC.

Use [PLACE] IN ART for works that are artistic representations of places or discussions of their treatment in art, e.g.,

CALIFORNIA IN ART.
NEW YORK (N.Y.) IN ART.
ROCKY MOUNTAINS IN ART.
BRAZIL IN ART.
MISSISSIPPI RIVER IN ART.

For other works, use --DESCRIPTION--VIEWS; --DESCRIPTION AND TRAVEL--VIEWS. (In artistic photography, the headings DESCRIPTION. . . are always used instead of [PLACE] IN ART).
Use [SUBJECT] IN ART for works that are artistic representations of subjects or discussions about their treatment in art, e.g.,

WOMEN IN ART.
ANIMALS IN ART.
PRIMITIVISM IN ART.
RURAL POOR IN ART.
KINGS AND RULERS IN ART.

Use the subdivision --PICTORIAL WORKS for those works that are not offered primarily for their artistic value.

Art collections	Use for either a personal or corporate original owner of an art collection, e.g.,

ROCKWELL, ROBERT F.--ART COLLECTIONS.

Biography	Do not use directly under the name of the artist. Assign an additional heading for the class of person to bring out biographical treatment, e.g.,

PAINTERS, FRENCH--BIOGRAPHY.

Caricatures and cartoons	Use under topics, events (excluding wars), corporate bodies, and class of person. For individuals, use CARTOONS, SATIRE, ETC.
Cartoons, satire, etc.	Use under individuals, excepting literary authors (then use PORTRAITS, ETC.), e.g., REAGAN, RONALD--CARTOONS, SATIRE, ETC.
Catalogs	[OBJECT]--CATALOGS. [KIND OF INSTITUTION]--CATALOGS [NAME OF INSTITUTION]--CATALOGS. [NAME OF INDIVIDUAL]--CATALOGS. For catalogs of exhibitions, use --EXHIBITIONS.
Catalogs and collections	Do not use for art objects.
Collection and preservation	Do not use for art objects.
Collectors and collecting	[OBJECT]--COLLECTORS AND COLLECTING. [INDIVIDUAL COLLECTOR]--COLLECTORS AND COLLECTING. e.g., ART--COLLECTORS AND COLLECTING. GREY, ABBY WEED--COLLECTORS AND COLLECTING.
Competitions	
Conservation and restoration	
Correspondence	See note under BIOGRAPHY.

Description--   Use under cities, parks, universities, mountain
Views   peaks, and other geographic areas for works
                    consisting exclusively or predominantly of views
                    of them, e.g.,

      PARIS (FRANCE)--DESCRIPTION--VIEWS.

Description   Use under names of regions or jurisdictions
and   larger than cities for works which consist
travel--Views   predominantly of views of them, e.g.,

      CALIFORNIA--DESCRIPTION AND
        TRAVEL--VIEWS.

Designs and   Use under architectural headings.
plans

Exhibitions   Use under objects, form, place, and corporate
                    bodies, e.g.,

      MEDALS--EXHIBITIONS.
      PAINTING, FRENCH--EXHIBITIONS.
      NEW YORK (N.Y.)--EXHIBITIONS.
      ART INSTITUTE OF
        CHICAGO--EXHIBITIONS.

Foreign
influences

History   History is not traditionally used under art for
                    subdivisions, e.g., --ART; --PORTRAITS, ETC.;
                    etc.

History and   Do not use in art; prefer the subject heading
criticism   ART CRITICISM, or the subdivision
                    --REVIEWS.

Iconography   Use for works consisting almost entirely of
                    portraits but also containing pictures of friends,
                    family, homes, results of creative activity, etc.
                    under names of individuals and classes of
                    people, e.g.,

      GOGH, VINCENT VAN,
        1853–1890--ICONOGRAPHY.
      PAINTERS--ICONOGRAPHY.

Influence	[NAME OF INDIVIDUAL]--INFLUENCE. [SACRED WORK]--INFLUENCE. [PARTICULAR ART FORM]--INFLUENCE. [MOVEMENTS]--INFLUENCE. [TYPE OF ORGANIZATION]--INFLUENCE. On whom or what this influence was brought to bear is unspecified and should be brought out under other subject headings.
Interviews	See note under --BIOGRAPHY.
Museums	[TOPIC]--MUSEUMS. [CITY]--MUSEUMS.
Photograph collections	[ORIGINAL OWNER; INDIVIDUAL OR CORPORATE]--PHOTOGRAPH COLLECTIONS. [NAME OF PUBLIC INSTITUTION]--PHOTOGRAPH COLLECTIONS. (If collection is unnamed)
Pictorial works	Use for works which consist exclusively or predominantly of illustrations under topical headings, e.g., AUTOMOBILES--PICTORIAL WORKS. For works about a topic represented artistically see [SUBJECT] IN ART.
Portraits	[CLASS OF PERSON]--PORTRAITS. If not issued for artistic value, use --PICTORIAL WORKS. Not to be used under the name of an individual.
Portraits, caricatures, etc.	Use under the names of individual persons or families likely to be caricatured—e.g., politicians, statesmen, rulers—who have lived after 1400 (if before 1400, use --ART.), e.g., CHURCHILL, WINSTON, SIR, 1874–1965--PORTRAITS, CARICATURES, ETC.

	For pictorial humor, use --CARTOONS, SATIRE, ETC.
Portraits, etc.	Use under the names of individual persons or families except statesmen, etc., for portraits or for portraits and caricatures of those persons, e.g.,
	PICASSO, PABLO, 1881–1973--PORTRAITS, ETC.
	For pictorial humor, use --CARTOONS, SATIRE, ETC.
Preservation	Do not use under art objects; prefer CONSERVATION AND RESTORATION.
Private collections	Use under kinds of objects for discussions of various privately owned collections, e.g.,
	SCULPTURE, DUTCH--PRIVATE COLLECTIONS.
Reviews	Use under types of artistic production for descriptive or critical works.
Technique	
Themes, motives	Use for general discussions of the themes occurring or possible in the form discussed, e.g.,
	ART, JAPANESE--THEMES, MOTIVES.

Fine arts items obviously come in forms other than books. For guidance in the description of these items, consult the appropriate chapters of *AACR2*. For graphic items, Elisabeth W. Betz's *Graphic Materials: Rules for Describing Original Items and Historical Collections* should be used along with *AACR2* Chapter 8.

The very nature of art is the realization of new concepts. One of the more problematic aspects of fine arts cataloging is that the classification schemes and subject headings cannot keep current with styles, movements, and techniques. When confronted with this dilemma by an item in hand, there are several options: (1) leave the item sitting on the shelf until an undetermined future date and hope that someone else will catalog it; (2) catalog the item, fitting it into the existing classification and subject headings as well as possible; or (3) establish local headings specific to the item. This problem exists in all disciplines and decisions must be made locally depending on urgency, institutional policy, and the standards of shared bibliographic utilities.

BIBLIOGRAPHY

Anglo-American Cataloging Rules. 2d ed. Chicago: American Library Association, 1978.

Betz, Elisabeth W. *Graphic Materials: Rules for Describing Original Items and Historical Collections.* Washington, DC: Library of Congress, 1982.

Dewey, Melvil. *Dewey Decimal Classification and Relative Index.* 19th ed. Albany, NY: Forest Press, 1979.

Immroth, John Phillip. *Immroth's Guide to the Library of Congress Classification.* 3d ed. by Lois Mai Chan. Littleton, CO: Libraries Unlimited, 1980.

LC Rule Interpretations of AACR2. Compiled by Sally C. Tseng. 1978–1984 ed. Metuchen, NJ: Scarecrow Press, 1985.

Library of Congress. Processing Services. *Cataloging Service Bulletin.* Washington, DC: Library of Congress, 1978–.

Library of Congress. Subject Cataloging Division. *Classification: Class N: Fine Arts.* 4th ed. Washington, DC: Library of Congress, 1970.

Library of Congress. Subject Cataloging Division. *Classification Schedules, Class N, Fine Arts.* Detroit, MI: Gale Research, 1984.

Library of Congress. Subject Cataloging Division. *Library of Congress Subject Headings: a Guide to Subdivision Practice.* Washington, DC: Library of Congress, 1981.

Library of Congress. Subject Cataloging Division. *Subject Cataloging Manual: Subject Headings.* Preliminary ed. Washington, DC: Library of Congress, 1984.

Salinger, Florence A. and Eileen Zagon. *Notes for Catalogers: a Sourcebook for Use with AACR2.* White Plains, NY: Knowledge Industry Publications, 1985.

Uniform Titles for Music Under *AACR2* and Its Predecessors: The Problems and Possibilities of Developing a User-Friendly Repertoire

by Don C. Seibert and Charles M. Herrold, Jr.

> The subject of uniform titles is one which bulks large in discussions of music cataloging.
>
> C.P. Ravilious[1]

Uniform titles have only begun to assume a prominent role in the cataloging of books since the adoption of *AACR2*. They have, however, long been an important feature of music cataloging. The reason for this lies in an important difference between books and music materials. The language of a book's title page is in most cases the same as the language of the text and that language will determine whether or not a particular book can be understood by a particular reader. Typical Americans going to their local libraries to find a copy of Tolstoy's *War and Peace* will not be interested to learn in the course of the search that the library owns a German edition with the title *Krieg und Frieden,* an Italian edition entitled *Guerra e pace,* or an edition with Tolstoy's original Russian title of *Volna i mir.* In fact, the typical patron will only be interested in an English-language edition with the familiar *War and Peace* on the title page.

The authors wish to extend special thanks to Joan Colquhoun and Lucinda Wells of the National Library of Canada for providing much helpful information about NLC's bilingual cataloging system.
1. "AACR2 and Its Implications for Music Cataloguing," *Brio* 16 (1979): 6.

On the other hand, a pianist going to the local library for a copy of Mussorgsky's *Pictures at an Exhibition* will be interested in a German edition with the title *Bilder einer Ausstellung,* a French edition with the title *Tableaux d'une exposition,* an Italian edition with the title *Quadri di una esposizione,* or even a Russian edition with the title *Kartinki s vistavki.* That is because music is in the universal language of notes, which remain the same regardless of the language of the title page and are equally useful no matter what country is the source of a printed edition. And while an editor's comments may be unreadable if in a language foreign to a particular musician, the composer's tempo indications (*moderato, presto* and the like) tend to be the same from edition to edition and to be in a common terminology (most often Italian) familiar to most musicians.

The same holds true for record borrowers. Listeners will be quite happy with a record having the jacket title of *Dornroschen* as long as it contains a fine performance of Tchaikovsky's *Sleeping Beauty.* They may not even care if a performance of a Janácek opera is sung in German or Czech if they are primarily interested in hearing the music.

It therefore becomes important for a library patron to be able to locate all the scores or recordings of a particular musical work regardless of title page or jacket title. If these are entered under the title assigned by the publisher or record manufacturer, they will be scattered through the alphabet under the composer's name. For example, to locate the various editions of *Pictures at an exhibition* mentioned above, a pianist would have to look under B, K, P, Q, and T. Actually, not being able to guess what other editions of the work a library might own (Polish? Spanish?), the performer would have to check every single entry under Mussorgsky in order to do a thorough serarch. (This would stretch to the snapping point the patience of all but the most determined users.) A library wishing to offer good service to its patrons must therefore provide a gathering point where all these editions may be conveniently located. Under *AACR1* and its predecessor, the Library of Congress Rules of 1949 (hereafter cited as LC–1949), that gathering point was [Pictures at an exhibition]. Under *AACR2,* that gathering point is [Kartinki s vystavki]. The change has been the cause of considerable controversy and will be discussed in some detail further on.[2]

2. Full citations for the three cataloging codes referred to in this paragraph are: *AACR1* = *Anglo-American Cataloging Rules: North American Text* (Chicago: American Library Association, 1967); LC–1949 = *Rules for Descriptive Cataloging in the Library of Congress* (Washington, DC, 1949); *AACR2* = *Anglo-American Cataloguing Rules,* 2d ed. (Chicago: American Library Association, 1978). In LC–1949, the gathering point for the various editions of a musical work was called a "conventional title," while in *AACR1,* this term was changed to "uniform title." A close comparison of the rules for formulat-

There are actually three types of gathering points or uniform titles. This article occupies itself mainly with brief descriptions of how each type was formulated under LC–1949 and *AACR1* and what changes occurred with *AACR2*. In addition, it offers some appraisals of the various formulations in terms of user convenience. Finally, it suggests a solution to the problems of user inconvenience which were present with LC–1949 and *AACR1* and seem to have been multiplied by*AACR2*. Along the way, there are occasional and hopefully mind-stretching digressions to consider the alternatives proposed by the International Association of Music Libraries (IAML) code of 1971[3] and to look at the French uniform titles supplied by the National Library of Canada to its French-speaking clientele.

Before plunging into the discussion, however, the authors would like to offer a brief, preliminary digression: What if something other than titles had been chosen as gathering points for the various editions of the same musical work? What if, instead of uniform titles, uniform numbers had been chosen? In carrying out such a scheme, opus numbers or thematic catalog numbers might be used when available. Otherwise, arbitrary numbers could be assigned to various works and classes of works. The advantage of such an approach would be its universal applicability. A numbering scheme, once agreed upon, would be just as convenient (or inconvenient) in the Soviet Union as in the United States.

Convenience, of course, is the key to the choice of names over numbers. Names are easier to remember. And in many, many instances, the name assigned by the composer and subsequently adopted as the uniform title is also the name familiar to the average user. These examples come easily to mind.

Appalachian spring
Nocturnes
Aïda
La valse

Of course, one might point out that when, under *AACR2,* readers are referred from a familiar title such as *Sleeping Beauty* to an unfamiliar one such as *Spâashchaâa Krasavâtsa,* they are no more inconvenienced than if referred to op. 66. The problem with a numbering scheme is that there would always be cross-references to use until patrons began to memorize the numbers, while with titles patrons often hit the right one, or at least the chosen one, on the first try.

---

ing these titles in the two earlier codes shows few essential differences, which makes the changes mandated by the current code, *AACR2;* all the more striking.

3. International Association of Music Libraries. International Cataloging Code Commission, *Code International de catalogage de la musique,* vol. 3, *Rules for Full Cataloging* (Frankfurt; New York: C.F. Peters, 1971).

Other reasons to opt for titles are that this parallels the approach long used for books, for which there are no established numbering schemes, and because titles draw together in one sequence all of a composer's works in one form. For instance, all of Beethoven's sonatas for piano, in collections and single issues, file adjacent to one another. Using opus numbers would scatter these works.

FORM TITLES

And now to the heart of the matter. Three types of uniform titles are used in the cataloging of music: form titles, collective titles, and distinctive titles. Form (or genre) titles are used for works in which the principal element in the title is the name of a type of composition, e.g., sonata, suite, rondo, etc. Qualifiers are usually present, most often one or more of the following:

> medium of performance: piano, violin, etc.
> numerical identification: no. 3; op. 6; K. 446, etc.
> key: A major, C # minor, etc.

Other qualifiers may shift the title to the category of distinctive or, in the case of nicknames, may be ignored. For example, *Rhapsody in blue* is considered to be a distinctive title, even though the form word "rhapsody" is present, while the nickname "Moonlight," as applied to Beethoven's piano sonata, is not included in the work's uniform title.[4]

When a title-page title such as *Dritte Sonata in H-moll, für Bratsche und Klavier, Op. 22,* is converted into a form title, the elements are rescrambled into a prescribed order and translated when necessary into their English equivalents. The above work would, under LC-1949 and *AACR1,* have the following uniform title.

> [Sonata, viola & piano, no. 3, op. 22, B minor]

Changes to such a title under *AACR2* would be slight. The form word would be given in the plural and the space/ampersand/space between viola and piano would be changed to comma/space.

---

4. An historical aside: LC–1949 required the addition of the medium of performance to a form title "if the title proper consists of (or in instrumental music *contains* [emphasis added]) the name of a type of musical composition" (p. 78). This resulted in uniform titles such as [Rhapsody in blue, piano & orchestra]. Although this provision was abandoned in *AACR1,* the Library of Congress continued to use such titles (if already established) until the implementation of *AACR2.* This is an example of so-called superimposition, which caused the impact of *AACR2* to be greater than it would have been had the 1967 code been adopted in full.

[Sonatas, viola, piano, no. 3, op. 22, B minor]

Other changes in form titles are noted briefly below.[5] In general, it may be said that LC–1949 and *AACR1* form titles were user-friendly and that the changes brought about by *AACR2* are, from the patron's point of view, minimal and unlikely to cause inconvenience. The one exception is the pluralizing of form words, which cause confusion. Picture someone who has retrieved the entry Jacob, Gordon, 1895– [Sonatas, trombone, piano]. Since the title on the score is *Trombone Sonata,* the searcher will most likely wonder why the uniform title implies the presence of two or more such works, or at the very least a multiplicity of trombone sonatas in the composer's oeuvre.

A word of background on this particular rule change is in order. Pluralization is obviously intended to facilitate computerized filing so that, for instance, an individual sonata would not file before collections of the composer's sonatas. It has a precedent in the IAML code, which recommends the use of the plural if (a) the composer is living (which boldly assumes that she or he will write another composition with that title), or (b) the composer has written more than one work in the form.[6]

The *AACR2* instructions are to: "give the name in the plural. . . unless the composer wrote only one work of the type."[7] Either approach to pluralizaton is bound to cause the cataloger grief, since the effort sometimes required to determine the uniqueness of a particular work can be formidable and time-wasting, especially if the composer is obscure. Furthermore, under *AACR2,* if a living composer does produce a second symphony, for example, the form name in the uniform title for the first work must be revised from singular to plural. The IAML code avoids that problem but generates another if the composer dies without subsequent issue.

---

5. Under LC–1949 and *AACR1,* the presence of the orchestra in a concerto was implied; under *AACR2,* it is stated. Thus, [Concerto, piano, no. 1, op. 23, Bb minor] became [Concertos, piano, orchestra, no. 1, op. 23, Bbminor]. Other modifications were: (1) the shift from [Quintet, woodwinds & horn] to [Quintets, winds] for the common ensemble of flute, oboe, clarinet, horn, and bassoon; (2) the complete listing of instruments in certain chamber music combinations, e.g., the change from [Quintet, clarinet & strings] to [Quintets, clarinet, violins, viola, violoncello]; and (3) the shift in position of the numeral indicating multiple instruments of one type, e.g., [Suite, 3 recorders] to [Suites, recorders (3)].

6. IAML, p. 29. The IAML code does, however, allow the singular form as an option.

7. *AACR2,* p. 475.

Pluralization is thus potentially misleading to the user and frequently painful for the cataloger. Its adoption by *AACR2* seems unwise, a case of going too far to accommodate the limitations of the computer. And there may be other ways of dealing with the problem it was designed to solve. For instance, certain online systems have truncation capabilities which allow a patron to retrieve singular and plural forms with one search. By using such a system, the patron may input "symphon+" and retrieve both "symphony" and "symphonies."

If we are stuck with plurals, however, the confusion might be eased if the punctuation between the form and medium statements suggested more in the way of separation. For instance, [Sonatas, trombone] implies that the words could be inverted to read Trombone sonatas, while [Sonatas: trombone] does not.

Before leaving the subject of form titles, it is intriguing to note the practice of the National Library of Canada (NLC), which must provide form titles for both its French- and English-speaking clienteles. NLC does its English cataloging according to *AACR2* and its French cataloging according to *Règles de catalogage anglo-américaines,* 2eme éd. (*RCAA2*).[8] NCL bibliographic records are distributed in CAN/MARC (Canadian equivalent of USMARC), which has the capability of carrying two uniform titles, two forms of the composer's name, and so forth, right down to complete equivalent bibliographic records for bilingual publications.

The French and English form titles provided by NLC are sometimes very similar because of cognates; e.g.:

Sonates, violon, piano, op. 14, la mineur
Sonatas, violin, piano, op. 14, A minor

But sometimes noncognates predominate:

Suites, hautbois, clavecin, ré majeur
Suites, oboe, harpsichord, D major

A German commentator has noted that this diversity would be a problem if catalog records from various sources were to be used together in international music bibliographies.[9] It was probably a desire to avoid the problem of language diversity in medium statements (and incidentally in designations of key) that led the IAML code to recommend that opus or thematic index numbers, when available, be used as the sole distinguishing elements with form

---

8. Montréal, ASTED, 1980.
9. Heinz Lanzke, "Die Musiksonderregeln zu den Regeln fur die Alphabetische Katalogisierung," *Fontes Artes Musicae* 29 (1982): 51.

titles,[10] as shown in the following examples.

Quartets. Op. 74
Concertos. K. 466

The IAML code, however, does recommend the use of medium statements if appropriate identifying numbers are not available. The application of these rules would produce some strange filing sequences, strange at least to patrons and librarians accustomed to Anglo-American procedures. The violin and piano sonatas of Hindemith, for example, would have uniform titles as follows under the IAML rules.

[Sonatas. Selections] (for all four sonatas)
[Sonatas. Op. 11, no. 1]
[Sonatas. Op. 11, no. 2]
[Sonatas, violin, piano, C]
[Sonatas, violin, piano, E]

Between the op. 11 sonatas and the other two would file all of Hindemith's various wind sonatas, e.g., [Sonatas, flute, piano]. Thus, the collocating function, the drawing together of similar works, which is such an attractive feature of form titles under the Anglo-American codes, would be severely compromised by implementation of the IAML recommendations.

COLLECTIVE TITLES

Collective titles are of two types. The first offers gathering places for collections of works of the same genre but with different individual titles. A few examples are given below, along with the French equivalents as they have been or most likely will be established by NLC according to *RCAA2*.

ballets	ballets
operas	opéras
oratorios	oratorios
songs	chansons
symphonic poems	poèmes symphoniques

This type of collective title, established under LC–1949 and *AACR1*, remains unchanged by *AACR2*.

---

10. IAML, p. 29. The more familiar sequence of form-medium-number is allowed, however, as an option.

The other type of collective title offers a gathering place for collections of works in the same medium of performance but with differing individual titles. This type underwent an important reformulation under *AACR2* which affected alphabetical position. Below are a number of representative medium titles as they formerly were and as they are now. For comparison, the corresponding French collective titles as formulated according to *RCAA2* are also shown.

LC-1949/*AACR1*	*AACR2*	*RCAA2*

For one or two specific instruments:

Works, piano	Piano music	Musique pour piano
Works, violin & harpsichord	Violin, harpsichord music	Musique pour violin, clavecin

For instruments of the same general type:

Works, keyboard instrument	Keyboard music	Musique pour instruments à clavier

For various combinations of solo instruments:

Works, chamber music	Chamber music	Musique de chambre

For large ensemble:

Works, band	Band music	Musique pour fanfare
Works, chorus	Choral music	Musique chorale
Works, orchestra	Orchestra music	Musique orchestrale

For broader categories still:

Works, instrumental	Instrumental music	Musique instrumentale

Works, vocal	Vocal music	Musique vocale

For a mixture of instrumental and vocal works:

Works. Selections	Selections	Extraits

For everything a composer wrote:

Works	Works	Oeuvre[11]

In appraising these various forms in terms of user convenience, it is important to point out that sometimes a patron or librarian must locate all of a library's editions of a particular work, whether they are separately published or recorded or in various types of collections. This might be to secure multiple copies of a score for class use, to locate various performances so that interpretive differences may be compared, or to find an alternative because a particular edition is in circulation. For example, the search chain for a user wishing to locate all of a library's editions and/or recordings of Bach's *Chromatic fantasie and fugue* would begin with the German cognate uniform title [Chromatische Fantasie und Fugue] and then proceed as follows.

Using LC-1949/AACR1 forms:	Using *AACR2* forms:
Works, harpsichord	Harpsichord music
Works, keyboard instrument	Keyboard music
Works, instrumental	Instrumental music
Works. Selections	Selections
Works	Works

The advantage of the *AACR2* sequence is that patrons would most likely guess the most specific heading, [Harpsichord music], by themselves. The disadvantage is that the other gathering places are scattered about the alphabet. Patrons would probably not think of looking for any of them unless instructed to do so. Nor is it likely that they would remember them all the next time a similar search need arose.[12]

The disadvantage of the *AACR1* sequence was that most patrons couldn't find any of these headings without assistance. The advantage was that they were all gathered together in one alphabetical spot, and

---

11. Singular is correct.

12. [Selections] is generally felt to be the medium title least likely to be spontaneously found or remembered by anybody.

that once this was pointed out to a patron, he or she was more likely to remember it in the future. By a happy accident of French grammar, the *RCAA2* medium titles are, with the exception of [Extraits] and [Oeuvre], gathered under "Musique" rather than scattered.

In the future, it seems likely that more and more library patrons will do their searching via online catalogs. Well-designed online catalogs are likely to provide access to individual words in uniform titles, and this capability should largely eliminate the problems caused by the alphabetical scattering of medium titles in English under *AACR2*. For example, a search combining the composer's name from the author field plus the word "music" from the uniform title field should retrieve all medium titles except [Selections] and [Works].

DISTINCTIVE TITLES

Distinctive titles are the ones left over after form and collective titles have been taken care of. Examples were given at the beginning of this article, e.g., *War and peace, Pictures at an exhibition.* Others are listed below.

Aïda
Die Zauberflote
Fidelio
Rodeo
Le tombeau de Couperin
Pini di Roma, etc.

AACR2 legislated minor and major changes involving distinctive titles. The minor ones are pesky but not controversial and are described briefly below.[13] As for the two major changes, the first of these in particular has been a principal source of the controversy generated by *AACR2* in music library circles. For this reason, the background for this change is described in considerable detail in the following paragraphs.

In establishing a distinctive title under LC–1949 and *AACR1*, a cataloger was to give general preference to the title of the first

---

13. For vocal works, *AACR1*'s modifying phrase "Piano-vocal score" was reduced to the less accurate but more frequently encountered term "Vocal score," which, by the way, had made a previous appearance in the British text of *AACR1*. *AACR2* changed the rules for the addition of language modifiers, bringing them into line with the rules for books. Under *AACR2*, language modifiers are used if a translation or a liturgical text is involved. Under *AACR1*, language modifiers were not used for full scores but always for vocal scores and librettos. *AACR2* prescribes the use of "Polyglot" when three or more languages are present, while under *AACR1* these were specified.

edition. There was, however, an important language limitation. If the first edition title was not in one of the common Western European languages (English, French, German, Italian, Spanish, Portuguese, or Latin), then "the title in most common use in the United States" was to be used.[14] This language limitation seems to have had a practical basis in the fact that many musicians, particularly those involved with vocal music, deal comfortably with Western European languages but not with Eastern European, let alone Japanese, Arabic, and other "non-garden variety languages" (to borrow a phrase of Phil Youngholm).[15]

However, in 1976 the Library of Congress abandoned this language limitation and started using original language titles for Eastern European operas and opera excerpts. (These were, of course, transliterated in the case of Cyrillic alphabet works.) The reasons were again practical. In the April 1975 *Music Cataloging Bulletin*[16] LC announced a plan to expand the number of composer-title tracings (sometimes called "analytics") it would provide on catalog copy for sound recordings. In the process of implementing this policy, LC staff found themselves having to establish uniform titles for arias from Eastern European operas and having a devil of a time deciding what form was in most common use in the United States.

The case of Tchaikovsky's sixth opera, variously known in this country as *Joan of Arc* and *The Maid of Orleans,* makes a useful example. The work's one famous excerpt is the heroine's first act aria, best known in a French version as "Adieu forêts." However, since under the then-current rules the opera had been given the English uniform title of [Joan of Arc], the aria was established under the excerpt title of "Farewell ye woods," apparently for linguistic consistency. This was, of course, inconsistent with the rule which said to use "the title in most common use in the United States." Even more perplexing was the problem posed by two other separately recorded excerpts (the first act prayer and the third act duet) which were little known and for which there were no well-established Western European language equivalents.

The LC staff had previously solved this problem by using a literal translation of the Russian. In the two instances mentioned above, the resulting uniform titles were as follows.

[Joan of Arc. Hymn]
[Joan of Arc. Scene and duet, Joan and Lionel, act 3]

---

14. *AACR1,* p. 235.
15. "Foreign-Language Musical Uniform Titles Required by *AACR2*," *U*N*A*B*A*S*H*E*D Librarian* 43 (1982): 31.
16. *Music Cataloging Bulletin* 6(4) (April 1975): 3.

That was one expedient way of dealing with the difficulty, even though the results once again might not qualify as titles "in most common use in the United States." At least these titles had a certain comfortable recognizability for English-speaking, non-Russian-reading patrons, and this in most American libraries would have considerable merit.

In early 1976, however, LC decided that it would no longer accept these compromises. Instead, it would use transliterations of the Russian for excerpt titles. And to avoid having excerpts in Russian and work titles in English, LC changed the work titles to Russian also. The first effects of this new policy appeared in the June 1976 *Music Cataloging Bulletin* with a crop of Russian transliterations. And in August,[17] new uniform titles made their appearance for the three *Joan of Arc* excerpts alluded to above.

[Orleanskaia deva. Ariia Ioanny]
[Orleanskaia deva. Gimm Ioanny]
[Orleanskaia deva. Stsena i duet Ioanny i Lionelia]

This change of policy by LC was subsequently reflected in *AACR2,* which dropped the Western European language bias of LC–1949 and *AACR1* and preferred original languages, no matter how exotic.[18]

AACR2 made one other major change involving distinctive titles. Consistent with the general goal of bringing music cataloging more closely in line with book cataloging, the first choice in establishing distinctive titles was to be the best-known title in the original language. Failing this, the second choice was to be "the composer's original title."[19] The guideline for establishing a best-known title comes from the general rule for uniform titles: it is to be the title "by which a work. . .has become known through use in manifestations of the work or in reference sources."[20] There is no guideline for establishing the composer's original title, leaving one to speculate on which is to be preferred: the title on the manuscript, that associated with the first performance or first edition, or whatever. One librarian has

---

17. *Music Cataloging Bulletin* 7(8) (August 1976): 2.

18. Although this article is primarily concerned with the public service aspects of uniform titles, it may be noted that the practicality of this policy change from the cataloger's viewpoint is even more evident when one considers not only opera arias but also the numerous short, obscure, or minor works that must be assigned uniform titles, particularly in the analytic cataloging of sound recordings. When Cyrillic titles are involved, the most economical procedure in terms of expeditious processing is to transliterate the original and move on, confidently, to other tasks.

19. *AACR2,* p. 474.

20. *AACR2,* p. 443.

commented whimsically on the need in this case for "spirit communications."[21] These are some uniform titles which have undergone radical changes as the result of the new rules.

LC-1949 AACR1	AACR2
Bach, Johann Sebastian	Bach, Johann Sebastian
[Aria mit 30 Veränderungen, harpsichord]	[Goldberg-Variationen]
[Concerti grossi]	[Brandenburgische Konzerte]
[Suites, harpsichord, S.806–811]	[Englische Suiten]
Chaĭkovskiĭ, Petr̂ Ilích	Tchaikovsky, Peter Ilich
[The nutcracker]	[Shchelkunchik]
Musorgskiĭ, Modest Petrovich	Mussorgsky, Modest Petrovich
[Pictures at an exhibition]	[Kartinki s vystavki]
Stravinskiĭ, Igor Fedorovich	Stravinsky, Igor
[Le sacre du printemps]	[Vesna svîashchennaîa]

Note that the three Russian composers' names changed with *AACR2* as well, from the transliterations used before 1981 to the forms encountered most often in English-language reference sources. For Mussorgsky and Stravinsky, the changes are minor. The Tchaikovsky citation offers one of the classic examples of *AACR2*'s inconsistencies: the composer's name has been shifted from the esoteric to the familiar, while the work's title has gone from the familiar to the esoteric and, for many American patrons, the unpronounceable.

In establishing uniform titles for the same six works, NLC uses the three Bach titles in the right-hand column for both its English- and French-speaking clienteles because these are the best-known titles in Bach's native German. As for the three Russian works, NLC's English entries would be the same as the LC entries cited above, but the French would be somewhat different.

Tchaïkovski, Piotr Illitch
[Ščelkunčik]

---

21. Quoted from p. 4 of a report on a poll conducted by the Working Group [later Round Table] on Alternative Approaches to Music Cataloging, a subgroup of the Music Library Association. The poll was distributed in the summer of 1983 to about 48 music librarians, of which 18 responded. The poll sought opinions on various changes in music cataloging brought about by *AACR2*.

Moussorgski, Modeste Pétrovitch
[Kartinki s vystavki]

Stravinsky, Igor
[Vesna svjaščennaja]

That is because, of course, the composers' names are based on French reference sources. Furthermore, the transliteration tables used in establishing distinctive titles for French bibliographic records are similar but not identical to those used for English bibliographic records. For the former, NLC employs the tables approved by the International Organization for Standardization; for the latter, both NLC and LC employ the American Library Association tables.

As a preliminary to appraising these various distinctive titles in terms of user-convenience, it seems appropriate to divide music library users into three broad categories: scholars; music students and professionals; music lovers and amateur performers. Of course, a considerable degree of overlap is inevitable.

It appears that original titles, be they the titles of first publication preferred by LC-1949/*AACR1,* manuscript titles, or whatever, are likely to have a strong appeal to scholars. Original titles have an attractive "purity" about them. "This is what the composer called it, and we should respect his wishes." Scholars are likely to be familiar with them already, or if not, would want to know them. Original titles, especially when they are esoteric, may even have a certain snob appeal.

Original titles may also have an educational value for music students and professionals. In the days of *AACR1,* it was perhaps of some value for a pianist or harpsichordist to be directed from *Goldberg variations* to [Aria mit 30 Veränderungen, harpsichord], and to learn in the process that the latter (except for the word "harpsichord") was Bach's own title for the work. And it also seems right that a voice student learning an aria from *The Magic Flute* should discover that the opera's original German title is *Die Zauberflöte.* Thus, original titles appear to be the best choice for scholars and a useful choice, if not the most convenient one, for performers and music students.[22]

---

22. Another argument in favor of original-language titles is their prominence in the major English-language music encyclopedia, the *New Grove Dictionary.* For example, the citation for Stravinsky's 1913 ballet reads: Vesna svyaschennaya (Le sacre du printemps) [The rite of spring (literally 'Sacred spring')]; Mussorgsky's *Pictures* is given as: Kartinki s vïstavki [Pictures at an exhibition], and so forth. Note that these transliterations are slightly different from those employed by LC, illustrating that problem once again.

Original titles are not likely to be the best choice for the third category of music library patrons—the music lovers and amateur musicians. Members of this group are least likely to be patient and/or sophisticated library users. They are the least likely to successfully negotiate a system of cross-references. For them, one would ideally like to keep the library system as simple as possible. For this group, the titles best known in their own country would be the most helpful and convenient. And, it must be admitted, this holds true for many music students and music professionals as well.

AACR2, with its preference for best-known titles in the original language, is actually a partial move in the general direction of offering better service to this large category of music library users. It is at its user-friendliest when the original language is English. It also is very helpful when the terms in the original language have English cognates. Thus, the three Bach uniform titles cited above are close in their *AACR2* forms to the common English equivalents, thus easily recognized and a big improvement over the *AACR1* forms in user-friendliness. On the other hand, the three Russian uniform titles are just the opposite.

One may reasonably ask: if best-known titles in the original language are now preferred over first edition or other forms of original titles, why not go all the way and use best-known titles in the country of the cataloging agency? Why settle for [Englische Suiten] when [English Suites] would suit the American, English, and English-speaking Canadian publics best of all?[23]

There are two reasons for not "going all the way." First, sticking to the original language eliminates the excerpt-title problem since these may simply be copies from first or scholarly editions of the works in question. Second, retaining the original language seems to satisfy the urge toward Universal Bibliographic Control or, more specifically, the desire to facilitate the international exchange of cataloging data by establishing universally acceptable uniform titles. Interestingly enough, however, the IAML code of 1971, presumably designed with international cooperation in mind, is rather more yielding on the language issue than is *AACR1*. Rule 2.421 of the IAML code, which covers distinctive titles, requires the use of the first-edition title (reflecting both LC–1949 and *AACR1*) unless the work is better

---

23. C.P. Ravilious, a critic of *AACR2*'s language rule, writes: "Rule 25.27A... opts for the composer's original title unless a later title in the same language is better known. In neither case is there an option to prefer a title in another language, even if the language of the original title is little known. There is perhaps a certain illogicality in the admission of familiarity as a criterion for choosing between versions of the title in the same language as against the disregard of the same principle when different languages are involved." (Op. cit: 8)

known by a later title (which anticipates *AACR2*).[24] However, the IAML code provides the alternative which *AACR2* lacks: the title may be translated into the language of the cataloging library or a "well-known" translation may be used.[25]

A NEW PRINCIPLE: DIVERSITY

The goal of establishing internationally acceptable uniform titles is understandable and even admirable, but it seems unrealistic and even unattainable in many cases. As has been shown throughout this article through French examples from NLC, form and collective titles require considerable translation to make them acceptable to another language group, and Russian distinctive titles may be transliterated differently depending on the language into which they are being transliterated.[26] As a Danish author has put it, there has been "no agreement on giving the same work the same name. . . .Even a filing title (uniform title) will not bring us to complete international unanimity, because filing titles may be following a common system, but they are written in the language of the cataloging agency."[27]

It may be safely said that the search for universal uniform titles, however commendable, will continue to founder on the rock of language differences. A similar situation exists within each nation: the search for uniform titles which serve equally well a diversity of library users will continue to encounter language difficulties. In this case, the problem is the difference between the various original-language titles associated with distinctively named works and the titles, generally in the language of the library's clientele, most likely to be recognized by that clientele.

The difficulty might be resolved by accepting the principle of diversity—a diversity of uniform titles for a diversity of publics. There are two ways in which this flexible arrangement might be

---

24. The code states that a thematic index is to be used in case of doubt, which, although an accepted practice in American cataloging, is not specifically articulated in the Anglo-American Rules.

25. IAML, p. 30.

26. The solution to the problem of international cooperation in the realm of uniform titles would seem to lie not in the establishment of universally acceptable forms, but rather in an international authority file which would permit easy conversion from the form preferred in one country to that preferred in another. Using such an authority file, a French cataloger could take a recording of *The Sleeping Beauty* cataloged in German with the German uniform title of [Dornroschen] and easily find the preferred French equivalent: [La belle au bois dormant].

27. Nanna Schiodt, "National and International Interaction in Music Cataloguing: A Danish Point of View," *International Cataloguing* 8 (1979): 21.

achieved. The first is through the exercise of local options. Local libraries might deviate, substituting uniform titles of their own choosing when LC titles seem unfriendly to local publics. Both *AACR1* and *AACR2* have urged this kind of flexibility.[28] However, there are two reasons why, in the mid-1980s, this recommendation is impractical. First, if different libraries use different filing titles for the same work, communication betwen those institutions for interlibrary loan purposes, etc. will be made more difficult. Second, to economize by maximizing the participation of clerical staff and to expedite the processing of new materials, many library administrations have decided to follow LC to the letter, thus minimizing the number of decisions that need to be made in cataloging any one item. As a result, urges to tailor-make local catalogs to suit local patrons have largely been thwarted.

The other way to promote a healthy diversity is to standardize it, to make alternatives available in cataloging copy that is distributed by large databases and to link these alternatives. CAN/MARC has the capacity for carrying two equivalent uniform titles in one bibliographic record. Perhaps USMARC and other MARC formats could be expanded to carry several uniform titles in one record. Six seems like a practical number, at least to start with. A field could be set aside for form titles, another for collective titles, and if there were four more, each could carry a specific kind of distinctive title: (1) titles of first publication, (2) composers' original titles if different, (3) best-known titles in the original language, and (4) best-known titles in the country of the cataloging agency.[29]

A local library with an online catalog could include access to all these alternatives in its search program. Thus, its public could use a diversity of title approaches and still find the items it seeks. A local library with a card catalog could choose the uniform title which best suited its clientele and make "see" references from the others.

A local library could reduce the need for professional decision making by ruling that a particular type of uniform title would be

---

28. *AACR2* states: "The need to use uniform titles varies from one catalogue to another and varies within one catalogue. Base the decision whether to use uniform titles in a particular instance on: (a) how well the work is known; (b) how many manifestations of the work are involved; (c) whether the main entry is under title; (d) whether the work was originally in another language; (e) the extent to which the catalogue is used for research purposes. Although the rules in this chapter are stated as instructions, apply them according to the policy of the cataloguing agency." (p. 441–42)

29. The MARC serials format provides a glimpse of this possibility in that it contains fields for different types of controlled titles (as distinguished from titles appearing in the publication); 210, abbreviated title (assigned by the International Serials Data System); 222, key title (assigned by the National Serials Data Program in the U.S.); and 242, translation of title by cataloging agency. A uniform title (240) may appear as well.

employed in all instances. A research library might choose always to use original titles; a public library might opt for titles best known by an English-speaking clientele. In the case of opera excerpts, a public library might prefer mixed-language uniform titles [The marriage of Figaro. Dovè sono?], while a research library would most likely take a purer stance.

In many cases, these various titles are present already as references in authority file records and would only require precise identification and tagging. Nevertheless, the task of establishing four uniform titles instead of only one might prove too burdensome for a national cataloging agency such as LC. In the United States, perhaps the Music Library Association would be willing to share the work. Maybe a special committee of expert catalogers could be appointed to collaborate with LC on multiple uniform titles, in much the same way that various institutions are now cooperating with LC in the creation of name-authority records.

As automation of music cataloging copy becomes ever more extensive, both in the form of online catalogs and of access to automated bibliographic and authority records through utilities, we need to consider the flexibility which this technology can provide. The controlled flexibility built into our current cataloging rules in the form of options need not be subordinated to the decisions which a national library makes primarily for its own catalog. The rest of us should be able to make decisions for the good of our own publics, and in the process draw on an authorized, official repertory of alternatives.

It's worth thinking about.

Cataloging Government Publications: An Access Perspective

by Ellen Gay Detlefsen

The information produced by a government entity—be it federal, state, local, international, or even intergovernmental—has been at once a headache and a delight for the librarian and information specialist. The delightful part comes when an elusive, vital, or unusual snippet of information or a necessary and crucial monograph is uncovered in the depths of the fearsome "government documents" collection; the headache happens when a librarian or information specialist, uninitiated into the different ways of handling these materials, faces the prospect of having to search for and use them. All too frequently, their care and handling are left (with a sigh of relief) to that individual who was bold enough to take a single "docs" course in library school, the result of which is presumably instant expertise with governmental information. Those unfamiliar with the world of government information assume that it is the source of last resort, and its advocates are viewed as "documents freaks," GODORT activists, or just slightly deranged. When the parent organization plans for library orientation, bibliographic instruction, public relations campaigns, and the like, too often the materials and services of the government information collection are left out entirely, or, if included, are relegated to a "special materials" section that unnecessarily provides an image of the materials as different, difficult, and avoidable. Even the physical space assigned to governmental information collections is often not inviting nor even convenient to users; many institutions have chosen to put these items and their caretakers out of sight (and out of mind). Average library users, when polled, often can't tell where in the building the materials are housed, and many, when asked, don't even understand that monographs, serials, maps, pamphlets, posters, audiovisuals, and databases from their governments can be used as effective sources of both daily and research information.

These barriers of location and administration notwithstanding, the greatest obstacle to the effective use of the wealth of information available in governmentally produced materials is the complete absence of data about them in the typical library catalog. If access to govenment information appears in the main catalog for an institution, chances are that it appears only in the form of guide cards that indicate, for a specific topic, "additional information is available in the Government Documents Collection." These guide cards do not often encourage individual users to enter the unfamiliar territory. They seldom, if ever, explain that the collection employs a different classification scheme, and for many current subjects (on which a variety of government information resources exist), no guide card may yet appear because someone forgot to make the extra effort to produce the necessary entry. These problems persist without regard to the format of the catalog itself. The absence of clues leading to the collection of government information is just as troublesome in COM or online catalogs as in the traditional card catalog.

The library literature on cataloging government publications is sparse, and most of it appears in journals devoted to government information. Calls for expanded cataloging are typically published in journals read only by government documents specialists and may rightly be considered as preaching to the converted. Occasionally, a technical services journal will run such a piece, but seldom are issues of access to government information raised in the periodicals commonly read by reference/public services/access services specialists. Until the entire universe of information professionals is aware of and comfortable with the daily use of government information, repeated efforts are necessary to make the reality of government information more apparent to both professionals and their clients.

One obvious way to increase understanding and use of government information is to provide better access to it in the standard tools that people use to find materials in libraries. One of the most familiar and moderately comfortable access tools for the public is the catalog. They often ascribe to it magical properties which the professionals who provide and care for it know to be inaccurate and misleading, but it remains the tool of choice for many individuals who believe it to be the key to the library's collections and to the universe of available knowledge. The problem for access specialists (whether they reside in technical services, reference services, or special collections) is to make the catalog truly reflect the materials available to the user. Changes in cataloging practice and use are now necessary if familiarity and use of government information are to increase. Any library or information collection can take at least some steps to improve access to government information. Some can take the giant steps necessary for total, integrated access to information regardless of its source.

In the realm of providing catalog access to government information, one can conclude that there are indeed "different strokes for different folks," and that it is probably best to consider the concerns of the depository library separate from those of non-depository libraries. Depository status accrues to a library when it agrees to accept free materials from a government or one of its agencies, and in return promises to provide housing, staffing, and service for the materials so acquired. In general, "depository library" most commonly refers to those libraries participating in the depository programs for federal materials that emanate from the US Government Printing Office (GPO) through library programs administered by the Superintendent of Documents. Other government agencies, on all levels, also provide depository services, but the major concern for most US libraries is with the depository program for US government materials. Those in charge of government information collections face at least three decisions in seeking to implement better cataloging access to the items under their purview: (1) to use a separate catalog, (2) to integrate entries for government information into the main or union catalog, but to maintain a separate physical space for the collection, or (3) to integrate both the materials and the catalog.

USING SEPARATE CATALOGS

Using a separate catalog is in fact what most depository collections already do. It is not in card, COM, or online format, but rather appears as a book catalog, the *Monthly Catalog of United States Government Publications*—that old warhorse from the GPO which now provides full MARC cataloging for the items available in depository and other libraries. While the current version is an improved model featuring fuller entries, OCLC numbers, and, for a large percentage of records, LC and Dewey classifications and LC subject headings, it still remains a difficult tool for the public to use as a catalog, particularly for those users more at home with the card catalog and its Dewey-esque 3 X 5s. The *Monthly Catalog* is further complicated by including all materials available from GPO, not just materials held by the depository library in which the user is trying to work, and by the fact that it also lists items not included in the depository program at all. Users and librarians alike are frustrated and challenged by a catalog that features information about a wealth of items that are not easily accessible. To make matters worse, the *Monthly Catalog* is not at all current, with lags of six or more months at times between receipt of materials from GPO and the appearance of cataloging entries, a situation which further frustrates the hapless user as well as the information professional sitting or standing on a pile of materials that are neither accessible nor shelvable.

The advent in the mid-1970s of GPO-prepared MARC records— a move that resulted not only in better entries in the *Monthly Catalog* but also in a tape that can be searched via DIALOG and BRS, thus enhancing awareness of government information for searchers and online specialists—proved a major change in improving catalog access. Libraries and their technical services staffs can now get cataloging copy for GPO publications as easily as they can for publications from any "regular" source. The presence of GPO MARC records in national bibliographic utilities and in tapes sold to vendors of catalog products allows for efficient and cost-effective production of document-related catalog entries for any type of catalog. The question that remains is "Why bother to do so?" Administrators and public access services staff and professionals must be convinced that including these entries in the main catalog offers advantages for all users of the library and that it overcomes the barriers imposed on government information by physical location, separate classification schemes, and fear.

INTEGRATING THE CATALOG

Some libraries, notably in universities with large depository collections, have chosen to move towards full integration of the catalog, using the OCLC records (from GPO MARC cataloging) as the main source for the entries and treating the subsequent records no differently from any other item added to the library's collections. Studies now indicate that individuals *do* use the materials in a government depository collection more, and that reference service routinely includes the use of government information in a way that was not possible when the materials and the catalog were segregated. The important goal of the depository program to get government information out to the people is more easily and readily met by such a system of access through the main catalog, and the library system can point with pride to a true union catalog reflecting the library's holdings more accurately than ever before. There is, of course, an increase in cataloging when the mass of government materials is added to the universe of materials needing to be entered and processed, but the automation of the cataloging function has made the task more feasible. The entries can be produced in whatever format suits the individual library's needs; changing to a COM or online catalog may be the ideal time to add full cataloging for the depository materials. Users becoming familiar with the new catalog format will enjoy access to a wider variety of materials.

For the most innovative of libraries, the decision to integrate the catalog may also lead to a decision to integrate the collection. Moving government publications from one central, if hidden, repository to merge with "regular" materials on the shelves will also increase patron access to government information. This move towards parity may be too bold, daring, and costly in both time and space for many libraries. For the library unable to physically integrate government publications, the decision to integrate the catalog may represent the best means by which to increase access and use.

Other libraries may decide for the third alternative, that of a separate catalog, but one which is compatible with the institution's main catalog and reflects only the holdings of government material selected for that particular collection. This separate catalog will, in essence, replace the *Monthly Catalog* as a location tool for the specific library but not as a bibliography of government publications. An occasional library has chosen to mount the entire *Monthly Catalog* tape as an online catalog and utilize interlibrary loan whenever the user asks for an item not in the collection. Commercial vendors, such as Marcive, will also tailor a catalog of government publications for individual libraries using GPO MARC tapes as the source.

Making the decision in a depository library to integrate the collection and catalog, integrate the catalog alone, or establish a separate catalog largely revolves around the issues of collection size, ease of access to cataloging copy or products, and, most important, the attitude of the decision-makers and power brokers toward government information and the necessity for easy access to it. Without an enthusiastic advocacy for such materials, the suggestion to integrate any or all aspects of the collection will have little effect. The library and its staff must be prepared to adopt a business-as-usual attitude and treat government information as normally as they treat information from any other source.

OPTIONS FOR NONDEPOSITORY LIBRARIES

For the nondepository library, there are also several options. These special, school, or small academic and public libraries may opt for full cataloging, selective cataloging, or no cataloging at all. For many of these organizations, the status quo is the strongest access position. Government publications are already treated exactly the same as any other material, being cataloged, processed, and circulated in the same manner as other library items. For these libraries, no real decisions are necessary in order to increase access. The only access issue may be in the acquisitions process, and professionals in these places need to assure themselves that they are in fact receiving or ordering all the useful government materials in the subject areas of interest to them. Many a special library is already familiar with government information; those with particularly strong collections may be in law and medicine; the former because the basics of their collection depend heavily upon government publications, and the latter because of programs like MEDOC (from the Eccles Health Science Library at the University of Utah) which offers basic resource information about government publications in health science fields while also providing basic cataloging data. These and other libraries—especially school and small public and academic institutions—secure their cataloging copy from a variety of sources, including OCLC, the LC Card Order service, and even CIP (which now occasionally appears in government publications). These facilities may also derive their cataloging information from the *Monthly Catalog,* in its print or database formats or from a vendor such as Marcive.

Other smaller libraries may choose to be selective in their cataloging of government publications, treating some of the heavier or more significant items as regular library materials—integrating them into both the collection and the catalog—and using cataloging copy from any of the various sources, be they bibliographic utilities, vendors, or versions of the *Monthly Catalog.* Monographs, series, serials, and similarly weighty items are then seen as ordinary library acquisitions and the ephemeral or less heavily used materials may simply be available in a vertical or information file.

The smallest libraries, or those whose collection development programs do not include heavy or even light reliance on government publications, may choose to do no cataloging whatever for those few government items that do surface in their collections. For these organizations, a subject-oriented vertical file into which one slips the occasional government pamphlet or journal may be the best answer to the issue of providing access to these kinds of materials. There is no immutable law declaring that all government publications (or any other materials) must be cataloged according to the narrowest reading of *AACR2,* and for many places the logical way to access these materials is to include them with other similar sources, however handled. The special or school library need feel no obligation to treat these items separately nor to catalog them fully.

While these remarks deal exclusively with the problems and pleasures associated with access to US federal publications, the same problems arise when dealing with state, local, international, and intergovernmental materials. Depository programs exist for many of these, but the missing factor is the *Monthly Catalog* with MARC records now available for federal materials. For these nonfederal items, the decision to integrate the catalog is essential, as no other reasonable means of access exists. Those bibliographies, handlists, checklists, and similar finding aids which accompany such publications do not usually provide MARC records nor anything closely resembling cataloging copy. Original cataloging (or the use of copy when it appears in a bibliographic utility) may be the only means to achieve integration and access. In all but the most sophisticated of research libraries, these collections are small and may be more easily considered for original cataloging and integration into the catalog, if not into the collection itself.

The real message of building an access perspective for government publications is to review on a collection-by-collection basis the manner in which access is provided. Such a review should reveal whether the problem of nonuse or underuse results from a behavioral issue among users or staff members who service users, from physical isolation which segregates the collection from the mainstream of library materials, or from a problem in providing catalog access to the materials themselves. If the problem is behavioral, both staff training and changes in access points may be necessary. If the problem is physical, then catalog access may be the only reasonable solution. If the problem lies in the catalog and the absence of entries, then some form of catalog integration may be required. In any of these scenarios, the move toward *in*clusion rather than *ex*clusion, and toward *inte*gration rather than *segre*gation, is appropriate. As libraries contemplate their technological futures, it seems a shame not to include in the materials and services being touted for the new information age those splendid (and oftimes unique) publications and data sources which emanate from a governmental agency or body.

RESOURCES

Roseann Boermann, and Susan A. Cady. "Government Publications in an Online Catalog: A Feasibility Study," *Information Technology & Libraries* 3 (4): 331–42 (December 1984).

Selma V. Foster, and Nancy C. Lufbarrow. "Documents to the People in One Easy Step," *New Horizons for Academic Libraries.* New York: K.G. Saur, 1979, pp. 453–55.

Peter S. Graham. "Government Documents and Cataloguing in Research Libraries," *Government Publications Review* 10 (1983): 117+.

Peter Hernon, and Charles R. McClure. *Public Access to Government Information: Issues, Trends, Strategies.* Norwood, NJ: Ablex, 1984.

Judy E. Myers. "The Effects of Technology on Access to Federal Government Information," *New Technology and Documents Librarianship.* Westport, CT: Meckler, 1983, pp. 27–41.

Judy E. Myers, and Helen H. Britton. "Government Documents in the Public Card Catalog: The Iceberg Surfaces," *Government Publications Review* 5 (3) (1978): 311–14.

Jan Swanbeck. "Federal Documents in the Online Catalog: Problems, Options and the Future," *Government Information Quarterly* 2 (2) (1985): 187–92.

Sharon Walbridge. "OCLC and the Government Documents Collection," *Government Publications Review* 9 (1982): 227–87.

Paula P. Watson, and Kathleen M. Heim. "Patterns of Access and Circulation in a Depository Documents Collection Under Full Bibliographic Control," *Government Publications Review* 11 (1984): 287+.

Appendices

Appendix A:
A Selection of Hennepin County Library Records for Online Databases

Compiled by Sanford Berman

AEROSPACE DATABASE (Online data base).
  DIALOG Information Services.

  updated biweekly.

  "Co-produced by the American Institute of Aeronautics and
Astronautics, Technical Information Service (AIAA/TIS) and the
National Aeronautics and Space Administration, Scientific and
Technical Information Branch."
  "Online version of two printed publications: International
Aerospace Abstracts...and Scientific and Technical Aerospace
Reports (STAR)."
  Dates from 1984.
  For computerized indexing services available at HCL, see
Librarian.

  1. Online data bases. 2. Astronautics--Abstracts. 3.
Astronautics--Bibliography. 4. Aviation--Abstracts. 5.
Aviation--Bibliography. 6. Space sciences--Abstracts. 7. Space
sciences--Bibliography. I. American Institute of Aeronautics and
Astronautics. Technical Information Service. II. United States.
National Aeronautics and Space Administration. Technical
Information Branch. III. DIALOG Information Services. IV. Title:
International Aerospace Abstracts. V. Title: Scientific and
Technical Aerospace Reports. VI. Title: STAR.

AGRICOLA (Online data base). DIALOG
   Information Services.

   updated monthly.

   "Cataloging and indexing database of the National Agricultural
Library."
   Dates from 1970.
   For computerized indexing services available at HCL, see
Librarian.

   1. Agriculture--Indexes. 2. Agriculture--Bibliography. 3. Online
data bases. I. National Agricultural Library. II. DIALOG
Information Services.

AMERICA: HISTORY AND LIFE (Online data
   base). DIALOG Information Services.

   updated quarterly.

   Prepared by ABC-Clio Inc.
   Covers "the full range of U. S. and Canadian history, area
studies, and current affairs."
   Often cited as AHL.
   Dates from 1964.
   For computerized indexing services available at HCL, see
Librarian.

   1. Online data bases. 2. United States--Indexes. 3.
Canada--Indexes. 4. Canada--History--Indexes. 5. United
States--History--Indexes. I. DIALOG Information Services. II.
ABC-Clio, Inc. III. Title: AHL.

ARTBIBLIOGRAPHIES MODERN (Online data
   base). DIALOG Information Services.

   updated quarterly.

   Prepared by ABC-Clio, Inc.
   "Contains references to all modern art and design literature in
books, dissertations, exhibition catalogs, and some 300
periodicals."
   Includes abstracts.
   Dates from 1974.
   For computerized indexing services available at HCL, see
Librarian.

   1. Modern art--Indexes. 2. Modern art--Abstracts. 3.
Art--Indexes. 4. Art--Abstracts. 5. Online data bases. 6.
Art--Periodicals--Indexes. I. DIALOG Information Services. II.
ABC-Clio, Inc. III. Title: ART BIBLIOGRAPHIES MODERN.

COMPUTER DATABASE (Online data base).
    DIALOG Information Services.

    updated biweekly.

    Produced by Management Contents, Inc.
    "Contains abstracts from...journals, newsletters, tabloids,
proceedings, and meeting transactions, as well as business books
and self-study courses, covering almost every aspect of computers,
telecommunications, and electronics." Also includes "full text
Tables of Contents for each issue of each journal covered."
    Dates from 1983.
    For computerized indexing services available at HCL, see
Librarian.

    1. Computers--Abstracts. 2. Telecommunication--Abstracts. 3.
Computers--Current awareness services. 4.
Telecommunication--Current awareness services. 5. Online data
bases. I. Management Contents, Inc. II. DIALOG Information
Services.

ENERGYLINE (Online data base). DIALOG
    Information Services.

    updated monthly.

    Prepared by Environment Information Center.
    "Machine-readable version of Energy Information Abstracts."
    Dates from 1971.
    For computerized indexing services available at HCL, see
Librarian.

    1. Online data bases. 2. Energy resources--Abstracts. 3. Energy
policy--Abstracts. I. DIALOG Information Services. II. Energy
Information Abstracts. III. Environment Information Center. IV.
Title: ENERGY LINE.

ENVIROLINE (Online data base). DIALOG
    Information Services.

    updated monthly.

    Prepared by Environment Information Center.
    Includes abstracts.
    Dates from 1971.
    For computerized indexing services available at HCL, see
Librarian.

    1. Online data bases. 2. Environmental policy--Abstracts. 3.
Environmental protection--Abstracts. 4. Environmental policy--Indexes.
5. Environmental protection--Indexes. I. DIALOG Information Services.
II. Environment Information Center.

ERIC (Online data base). DIALOG
    Information Services.

    updated monthly.

    "Complete database on educational materials from the Educational
Resources Information Center."
    Consists of Resources in Education and Current Index to Journals
in Education.
    Dates from 1966.
    For computerized indexing services available at HCL, see
Librarian.

    1. Online data bases. 2. Education--Indexes. 3.
Education--Abstracts. 4. Education--Periodicals--Indexes. I.
DIALOG Information Services. II. Title: Resources in Education.
III. Title: Current Index to Journals in Education. IV. Educational
Resources Information Center.

FOODS ADLIBRA (Online data base).
    DIALOG Information Services.

    updated monthly.

    Prepared by Komp Information Services.
    "Information on the latest developments in food technology and
packaging."
    Includes abstracts.
    Dates from 1974.
    For computerized indexing services available at HCL, see
Librarian.

    1. Food industry and trade--Abstracts. 2. Food
preparation--Abstracts. 3. Online data bases. I. DIALOG Information
Services. II. Komp Information Services. III. Title: ADLIBRA FOODS.

FOUNDATION GRANTS INDEX (Online data
    base). DIALOG Information Services.

    updated bimonthly.

    Prepared by Foundation Center.
    "Contains information on grants awarded by...major American
philanthropic foundations, representing all records from the Foundation
Grants Index section of the bimonthly Foundation News."
    Dates from 1973.
    For computerized indexing services available at HCL, see
Librarian.

    1. Grants--Indexes. 2. Online data bases. I. DIALOG Information
Service. II. Foundation News. III. Foundation Center, New York
City.

GPO MONTHLY CATALOG (Online data
    base). DIALOG Information Services.

    updated monthly.

    "Machine-readable equivalent of the printed Monthly Catalog of
United States Government Publications."
    Dates from July 1976.
    For computerized indexing services available at HCL, see
Librarian.

    1. Online data bases. 2. United States--Government
publications--Catalogs. 3. United States--Government
publications--Bibliography. I. DIALOG Information Services. II.
United States. Government Printing Office. III. Title: Monthly
Catalog of United States Government Publications. IV. Title:
Government Printing Office Monthly Catalog. V. Title: United States
Government Monthly Publications Catalog.

HEALTH PLANNING AND ADMINISTRATION
    (Online data base). DIALOG
    Information Services.

    updated monthly.

    Produced by National Library of Medicine.
    "Contains references to nonclinical literature on all aspects of
health care planning and facilities, health insurance, and the
aspects of financial management, personnel administration, manpower
planning and licensure and accreditation which apply to the
delivery of health care."
    Dates from 1975.
    For computerized indexing services available at HCL, see
Librarian.

    1. Health planning--Indexes. 2. Health planning--Bibliography.
3. Health services administration--Indexes. 4. Health services
administration--Bibliography. 5. Online data bases. I. DIALOG
Information Services. II. United States. National Library of
Medicine.

HISTORICAL ABSTRACTS (Online data
    base). DIALOG Information Services.

    updated quarterly.

    Prepared by ABC-Clio, Inc.
    "Abstracts and indexes the...periodical literature in history
and the related social sciences and humanities."
    Dates from 1973.
    For computerized indexing services available at HCL, see
Librarian.

    1. History--Abstracts. 2. Online data bases. I. DIALOG
Information Services. II. ABC-Clio, Inc.

INFOGLOBE (Online data base). New
    York Times Information Service.

"Full text of articles in Toronto Globe and Mail from
November 14, 1977. Excludes advertisements, weather reports, puzzles
and comics."
For computerized indexing services available at HCL, see
Librarian.

1. Toronto Globe and Mail--Indexes. 2. Current
events--Periodicals. 3. Newspapers--Toronto. 4. Online data bases.
5. Current events--Periodicals. 6. Newspapers--Indexes. 7.
Canada--Indexes. 8. Canada--Periodicals.

I. New York Times Information Service. II. Title: INFO GLOBE.

INFORMATION SCIENCE ABSTRACTS (Online
    data base). DIALOG Information Services.

updated bimonthly.

Produced by IFI/Plenum Data Company.
Includes "indexing and abstracts for journal articles, patents,
proceedings, monographs, government documents and reports, series
and other publications."
Dates from 1966.
For computerized indexing services available at HCL,
see Librarian.

1. Online data bases. 2. Information science--Abstracts. I.
IFI/Plenum Data Company. II. DIALOG Information Services.

LEGAL RESOURCE INDEX (Online data
    base). DIALOG Information Services.

updated monthly.

Prepared by Information Access Corporation.
"Provides...indexing of...key law journals and...law newspapers
plus legal monographs and government publications from the Library
of Congress MARC database."
Dates from 1980.
For computerized indexing services available at HCL, see
Librarian.

1. Law--Indexes. 2. Judicial system--Indexes. 3. Online data
bases. 4. Law--Periodicals--Indexes. I. DIALOG Information
Services. II. Information Access Corporation.

MLA BIBLIOGRAPHY (Online data base).
   DIALOG Information Services.

   updated annually.

   "Comprehensive bibliography of humanistic studies produced...by
the Modern Language Association."
   Dates from 1970.
   For computerized indexing services available at HCL, see
Librarian.

   1. Online data bases. 2. Humanities--Bibliography. 3.
Linguistics--Bibliography. 4. Literature--Bibliography. I. DIALOG
Information Services. II. Modern Language Association.

MAGAZINE INDEX (Online data
   base). DIALOG Information Services.

   updated monthly.

   Prepared by Information Access Corporation.
   Scope: "general magazines."
   Dates from 1976.
   Frequently cited as MI.
   For computerized indexing services
available at HCL, see Librarian.

   1. Periodicals--Indexes. 2. Online data bases. I. DIALOG
Information Services. II. Information Access Corporation. III.
Title: MI.

PAIS INTERNATIONAL (Online data
   base). DIALOG Information Services.

   updated quarterly.

   "Contains the records from the printed PAIS Bulletin and the
PAIS Foreign Language Index."
   Dates from 1976.
   For computerized indexing services available at HCL, see
Librarian.

   1. Online data bases. 2. Current events--Indexes. 3. Social
sciences--Indexes. 4. Policy sciences--Indexes. 5. Current
events--Bibliography. I. DIALOG Information Services. II. Title:
PAIS INTERNATIONAL. III. Title: PUBLIC AFFAIRS INFORMATION SERVICE
INTERNATIONAL. IV. Title: PAIS Bulletin. V. Title: PAIS Foreign
Language Index.

PHILOSOPHER'S INDEX (Online data
    base). DIALOG Information Services.

    updated quarterly.

    Prepared by Philosophy Documentation Center.
    "Indexing and abstracts."
    Dates from 1940.
    For computerized indexing services available at HCL, see
Librarian.

    1. Online data bases. 2. Philosophy--Abstracts. I. DIALOG
Information Services. II. Philosophy Documentation Center.

PSYCINFO (Online data base). DIALOG
    Information Services.

    updated monthly.

    Prepared by American Psychological Association.
    "Formerly PSYCHOLOGICAL ABSTRACTS."
    Dates from 1967.
    For computerized indexing services available at HCL, see
Librarian.

    1. Online data bases. 2. Psychology--Abstracts. I. DIALOG
Information Services. II. American Psychological Association. III.
Title: PSYCHOLOGICAL ABSTRACTS. IV. Title: PSYCH INFO. V. Title:
PSYCHOLOGY INFO.

RELIGION INDEX (Online data base).
    DIALOG Information Services

    updated monthly

    "Produced by the American Theological Library Association
Religion Indexes."
    "Online version of...Religion Index One: Periodicals (formerly,
Index to Religious Periodical Literature). Religion Index Two:
Multi-Author Works (RIT), Research in Ministry (an index to Doctor
of Ministry theses and reports), and numerous selected
bibliographies."
    Dates from 1949.
    For computerized indexing services available at HCL, see
Librarian.

    1. Online data bases. 2. Religion--Abstracts. 3.
Religions--Abstracts. 4. Religion--Bibliography. 5.
Religions--Bibliography. I. DIALOG Information Services. II.
American Theological Library Association Religion Indexes. III.
Title: Religion Index One: Periodicals. IV. Title: Religion Index
Two: Multi-Author Works. V. Title: Index to Religious Periodical
Literature. VI. Title: Research in Ministry.

ROBOTICS INFORMATION (Online data
    base). BRS.

    updated monthly.

    Produced by Corporate Information Center, Cincinnati Milacron
Industries. Covers English-language and selected foreign literature
on the technical and business aspects of robotics.
    Dates from 1980, "with selected coverage from 1970."
    For computerized indexing services available at HCL, see
Librarian.

    1. Online data bases. 2. Robotics--Bibliography. 3.
Robotics--Indexes. I. Cincinnati Milacron Industries. Corporate
Information Center. II. BRS.

SCISEARCH (Online data base). DIALOG
    Information Services.

    updated monthly.

    "Index to the literature of science and technology prepared by
the Institute for Scientific Information."
    Dates from 1970.
    For computerized indexing services available at HCL, see
Librarian.

    1. Online data bases. 2. Science--Abstracts. 3.
Technology--Abstracts. I. DIALOG Information Services. II.
Institute for Scientific Information. III. Title: SCI SEARCH. IV.
Title: SCIENCE SEARCH.

SOCIAL SCISEARCH (Online data base).
    DIALOG Information Services.

    updated monthly.

    Prepared by Institute for Scientific Information.
    Dates from 1972.
    For computerized indexing services available at HCL, see
Librarian.

    1. Online data bases. 2. Social sciences--Indexes. I. DIALOG
Information Services. II. Institute for Scientific Information. III.
Title: SOCIAL SCIENCE SEARCH. IV. Title: SOCIAL SCI SEARCH.

Appendix B: A Selection of Hennepin County Library Form Headings for Periodicals

Compiled by Sanford Berman

AFRO-AMERICAN
    PERIODICALS
ASIAN-AMERICAN
    PERIODICALS

"BEAT" PERIODICALS
CATHOLIC PERIODICALS
CHICANO PERIODICALS
CHILDREN'S PERIODICALS
CHRISTIAN PERIODICALS

FAN MAGAZINES
FASHION MAGAZINES
FEMINIST PERIODICALS
FILM PERIODICALS
FOREIGN-LANGUAGE
    PERIODICALS
FRENCH-LANGUAGE
    PERIODICALS

GAY PERIODICALS
GENERAL MAGAZINES
GERMAN-LANGUAGE
    PERIODICALS

HUMOR MAGAZINES

ILLUSTRATED
    PERIODICALS

JEWISH PERIODICALS

KOREAN-LANGUAGE
    PERIODICALS

LABOR PERIODICALS
LARGE PRINT
    PERIODICALS
LESBIAN PERIODICALS
LITTLE MAGAZINES

MEN'S PERIODICALS
MINNESOTA LITTLE
    MAGAZINES
MYSTERY MAGAZINES

NATIVE AMERICAN
    PERIODICALS
NAZI PERIODICALS
NEWAVE COMIX

ONLINE PERIODICALS

PERIODICALS--SPECIAL
  ISSUES
POLITICAL PERIODICALS
PRISON PERIODICALS
PROTESTANT PERIODICALS

RELIGIOUS NEWSPAPERS
  AND PERIODICALS
RUSSIAN-AMERICAN
  PERIODICALS

RUSSIAN-LANGUAGE
  PERIODICALS

SEX MAGAZINES
SPY MAGAZINES

TEENAGERS' PERIODICALS

UNDERGROUND COMIX

WOMEN'S PERIODICALS

NOTE: Unsubdivided headings are only assigned to actual periodical titles in the HCL collection. However, the forms may also be applied—with subheads—to non-serial works, e.g.:

"BEAT" PERIODICALS--BIBLIOGRAPHY
SEX MAGAZINES--HISTORY AND CRITICISM
UNDERGROUND COMIX--COLLECTORS AND COLLECT-
  ING
WOMEN'S PERIODICALS--DIRECTORIES

Appendix C: A Selection of Hennepin County Library Subject Headings for Children's Material

Compiled by Sanford Berman

ABSENT-MINDEDNESS
AEROBIC DANCING FOR
   CHILDREN
ALONENESS
ALPHABET SONGS
ANNOYANCE
ANTICIPATION

BAD LUCK
BEDTIME
BEST FRIENDS
BILINGUAL MATERIALS
BOOK REPORTS
BOSSINESS
BOY DETECTIVES
BOY/GIRL RELATIONS
BROWNIES AND ELVES
BULLYING AND BULLIES
BUNGLING AND
   BUNGLERS
BUSY PARENTS

CANDY STRIPERS
CAUTIONARY TALES AND
   VERSE

CAUTIOUSNESS
CHAOS
CHASES
CHILD ADVENTURERS
CHILD ASTRONAUTS
CHILD ATHLETES
CHILD BALLET DANCERS
CHILD CELEBRITIES
CHILD COWHANDS
CHILD DANCERS
CHILD DETECTIVES
CHILD ENTREPRENEURS
CHILD FASHION MODELS
CHILD FILMMAKERS
CHILD HEROES AND
   HEROINES
CHILD HOSTAGES
CHILD INVENTORS
CHILD JOURNALISTS
CHILD MUSICIANS
CHILD PEACE ACTIVISTS
CHILD PSYCHICS
CHILD SCIENTISTS
CHILD SOLDIERS
CHILD TEXTILE WORKERS

CHILD WHEELCHAIR
    USERS
CHILD WITNESSES
CHILDREN AND
    COMPUTERS
CHILDREN AND DENTISTS
CHILDREN AND DOCTORS
CHILDREN AND DOGS
CHILDREN AND
    EYEGLASSES
CHILDREN AND
    GARDENING
CHILDREN AND HORSES
CHILDREN AND
    HOUSEHOLD CHORES
CHILDREN AND MOVING
CHILDREN AND NUCLEAR
    WARFARE
CHILDREN AND PETS
CHILDREN AND SENIORS
CHILDREN AND SHOPPING
CHILDREN OF ARTISTS
CHILDREN OF CELEBRITIES
CHILDREN OF TEACHERS
CHILDREN OF
    UNEMPLOYED
    PARENTS
CHILDREN'S CHANTS
CLEVERNESS
COMING-OF-AGE STORIES
CORETTA SCOTT KING
    AWARD BOOKS
COUNTING SONGS
CRITICIZING
CUMULATIVE TALES

DETERMINATION
    (PERSONAL QUALITY)
DIRTINESS
DISABLED CHILDREN'S ART
DISCOURTESY
DISGUISES
DISNEY CHARACTERS
DISOBEDIENCE
DOG DETECTIVES

EASY AND DIFFICULT
    THINGS
EIGHTH-GRADERS
ENCHANTMENT
EXAGGERATION
EXCITEMENT

FAMILY PROBLEMS
FIFTH-GRADERS
FIRST DAY IN SCHOOL
FIRST-GRADERS
FLYING CARPETS
FOSTER CHILDREN
FOURTH-GRADERS
FRECKLES
FUNK MUSIC
FUNNY CARS

GAY CHILDREN
GAY TEENAGERS
GIRL DETECTIVES
GNOMES
GOBLINS
GOLDEN KITE AWARD
    BOOKS
GOOD LUCK

HANDICRAFT FOR
    CHILDREN
HEAVY METAL MUSIC
HIDDEN-PICTURE BOOKS

IMAGINARY PLAYMATES
INDEPENDENCE
    (PERSONAL QUALITY)
INDIFFERENCE (PERSONAL
    QUALITY)
INNER CITY
INNER CITY CHILDREN
INNER CITY SCHOOLS
INSENSITIVITY

JOKES

KNOW-IT-ALLS
KWANZA·

LESBIAN TEENAGERS
LIFT-THE-FLAP BOOKS
LIKES AND DISLIKES
LOOK-ALIKES
LOST CHILDREN
LOST DOGS

MAKING FRIENDS
MEMORIES
MISFITS (PERSONS)
MIX-AND-MATCH BOOKS
MOVING TO A NEW
    APARTMENT [CITY,
    COUNTRY,
    NEIGHBORHOOD,
    STATE]
MULTICULTURAL
    MATERIALS
MULTICULTURAL SONGS
MULTISENSUAL
    MATERIALS

NEW BABY IN FAMILY
NINTH-GRADERS
NONRACIST CHILDREN'S
    LITERATURE
NONSEXIST CHILDREN'S
    LITERATURE
NOSINESS

ONE-CHILD FAMILY
OPPOSITES
OVERNIGHT VISITS
OVERWEIGHT CHILDREN
OVERWEIGHT TEENAGERS

PAPER ROUTES
PARENT-SEPARATED
    CHILDREN
PEACE EDUCATION
    MATERIALS
PEANUTS CHARACTERS
PESTS (PERSONS)
PLAYING DOCTOR
PLAYING DOLLS
PLAYING HOSPITAL
PLAYING HOUSE

PLAYING SCHOOL
PLOT-YOUR-OWN STORIES
POP-UP CARDS, BOOKS,
    ETC.
PRESCHOOLERS'
    SOFTWARE
PRETENDING
PROTECTIVENESS

RAINY DAYS
READER PARTICIPATION
    BOOKS
RIGHT AND LEFT
    (DIRECTIONS)

SCHOOL RIDDLES
SCRATCH AND SNIFF
    BOOKS
SECOND-GRADERS
SECRETS
SECURITY BLANKETS
SELFISHNESS
SEPARATED FRIENDS,
    RELATIVES, ETC.
SESAME STREET
    CHARACTERS
SEVENTH-GRADERS
SHOUTING
SHOW-OFFS
SILLINESS
SIXTH-GRADERS
SLEEPINESS
SMALLNESS AND BIGNESS
SOLVE-IT-YOURSELF
    MYSTERY STORIES
SPLIT-PAGE BOOKS
STEPBROTHERS AND
    STEPSISTERS
SUPERHERO TELEVISION
    PROGRAMS
SURPRISE PARTIES

TALKATIVENESS
TALLNESS AND SHORTNESS
TEASING
TEENAGE BOYS
TEENAGE GIRLS

TEENAGERS AND MOVING
TEENAGERS AND NUCLEAR
   WARFARE
TENTH-GRADERS
TEXTURED BOOKS
THIRD-GRADERS
TRAIN RIDES
TRANSFORMATIONS
   (MAGIC)

UNKINDNESS
UNREASONABLENESS
UNSELFISHNESS
UP AND DOWN
   (DIRECTIONS)

WHISPERING
WICKEDNESS
WORKING PARENTS
WORST (CONCEPT)

Index

Compiled by Sanford Berman